CLAUDE GOLDSMID MONTEFIORE
ON THE ANCIENT RABBIS

BROWN UNIVERSITY
BROWN JUDAIC STUDIES

Edited by
Jacob Neusner
Ernest S. Frerichs
Richard S. Sarason
Wendell S. Dietrich

Number 4

CLAUDE GOLDSMID MONTEFIORE
ON THE ANCIENT RABBIS
THE SECOND GENERATION OF REFORM
JUDAISM IN BRITAIN

by
Joshua B. Stein

SCHOLARS PRESS
Missoula, Montana

CLAUDE GOLDSMID MONTEFIORE
ON THE ANCIENT RABBIS
THE SECOND GENERATION OF REFORM
JUDAISM IN BRITAIN

by
Joshua B. Stein

Published by
SCHOLARS PRESS
for
Brown University

Distributed by

SCHOLARS PRESS
Missoula, Montana 59806

CLAUDE GOLDSMID MONTEFIORE
ON THE ANCIENT RABBIS
THE SECOND GENERATION OF REFORM
JUDAISM IN BRITAIN

by
Joshua B. Stein

Library of Congress Cataloging in Publication Data
Stein, Joshua B
  Claude Goldsmid Montefiore on the ancient
Rabbis.

  (Brown Judaic studies ; no. 4)
  Bibliography: p.
  Includes index.
  1. Montefiore, Claude Joseph Goldsmid, 1858-
1938. 2. Rabbis. I. Title. II. Series.
BM755.M58S75   296.6'1   77-13194
ISBN 0-89130-190-9 pbk.

Printed in the United States of America
1 2 3 4 5

Printing Department
University of Montana
Missoula, Montana 59812

5476 UM Printing Services

TO MY PARENTS

TABLE OF CONTENTS

PREFACE

Claude Goldsmid Montefiore has never been the subject of serious scholarly analysis. This short study is a first step to remedy this situation. A *Festschrift* was compiled in his honor in 1929 (*Speculum Religiones*); in 1940 a rather chatty biography, based on his letters, was put together by his cousin Lucy Cohen (*Some Recollections of Claude Goldsmid Montefiore*). Starting in 1956, a series of Montefiore lectures has been delivered at the University of Southampton, England; he generally receives mention in books which deal with Jewish Reform, but that is the extent of the attention he has received thus far. Much of Montefiore's thought is not original. Much of it is aimed at a popular audience. Much of it is written in an unfortunate style. All of this probably accounts for the lack of attention he has received to date. Yet, as I shall show, Montefiore did accomplish a great deal, and he did contribute something new.

A man of remarkable energy, Montefiore was the prime mover in the establishment of Liberal Judaism in Britain. He codified its doctrines and spread its tenets. Liberal Judaism, as Montefiore conceived it, is based on the practices of Israel Jacobson, the theories of Samuel Holdheim and Abraham Geiger, and the experiences of the Reform Movement in Britain. Montefiore was not content, however, merely to adapt previous reform. He also added new doctrines of his own. These include the beliefs that Greek and Christian ideas must be absorbed into modern Judaism and that Rabbinic ethics are still of enormous value in the modern world. Indeed it will be the central argument in the pages which follow that throughout his long life Montefiore wrote about the Rabbis of antiquity with the distinct purpose of shaping and advancing Liberal Judaism.

We first attend to Montefiore's religion. His religious concerns are then shown to be the basis of his writings on the Rabbis. Finally, we test our conclusions with respect to Rabbinic conceptions of God and the Law as they appear in *A Rabbinic Anthology*. Rabbinic attitudes towards both these subjects were of particular interest to Montefiore and *A Rabbinic Anthology*, as Montefiore's last, and possibly most enduring work, provides us with his thoughts at their highest development.

It still remains necessary to devote similar studies to Montefiore's attitudes on the Old Testament, the New Testament, Greek philosophy and Zionism before it can be said that Montefiore's contribution to modern Judaism is fully understood. Thus in one way at least, this study is merely the opening phase of a complete review of Montefiore's achievements and methods. Attention will be devoted in these pages to Montefiore's views on the Greeks and early Christianity as they affect his views on Liberal Judaism and the Rabbis, but not as separate entities in and of themselves. When scholars continue the research begun here, I have little doubt that Montefiore's tendentious nature will again be seen to play as prominent a role as in those works which deal with the Rabbis. Montefiore was not an idealogue; that will be demonstrated in these pages; he was, however, a man with a purpose which never escaped him. He wrote to lead his readers to what he considered to be the right road to God--Liberal Judaism.

I am indebted to the following people for their assistance. Professor Jacob Neusner of Brown University directed this project in its original thesis form. His scholarly and stylistic improvements are reflected throughout. My wife, Becky, typed several versions of the manuscript without complaint, and supplied great moral and grammatical aid. Professor Mary Finger copy-edited the final draft, contributing generously of her time and skill. To each I

am grateful.   I am also indebted to the Max Richter
Foundation for a much needed grant to help defray the
costs of publication.

Joshua B. Stein
May 12, 1977
Bristol, Rhode Island

INTRODUCTION

W. R. Matthews holds that while Claude Montefiore "had his presuppositions and firm convictions, he never wrote as a partizan or employed learning to buttress a preconceived opinion."[1] The truth is just the opposite. Montefiore (1858-1938) published eighteen books and nearly one hundred shorter items with the specific intention of defining, defending and spreading Liberal Judaism.[2] As he conceived it, this new Judaism was to be much more than simply the British branch of the Jewish Reform Movement. What separates British Liberal, from German Reform, Judaism is Montefiore's grafting onto the latter elements of Hellenistic philosophy, Christianity and, as I shall show, aspects of Solomon Schechter's Conservative Judaism. Additionally, Montefiore seemed to search for a *via media* between his Judaism and the enlightened Orthodoxy which was the prevalent Anglo-Judaism of his day.[3]

Montefiore's policy, with respect to the Rabbis of antiquity, was to judge them by the standards of his new faith. When their writings could be shown to fit the new pattern, he praises them. When Rabbinic attitudes are out of touch with the new doctrine, he chides them. Generally speaking, this pattern produces praise for *Midrash* and *Aggadic* ethics and condemnation of *Halakhah*. Unfortunately, however, since Liberal Judaism draws from so many sources, Montefiore is frequently forced to distort the ancients in order to make his points. As a result, on occasion he contradicts himself or finds himself trying to defend or even to pass off untenable positions. Similarly, since he writes for two different audiences, Jewish and Christian, Montefiore is often in the position of having to tailor his facts and theories to suit his readers' assumed preconceptions. Consequently, much that he writes is tendentious in nature and not purely objective as the Reverend Matthews would have us believe.

1

While Montefiore's writings must be viewed within
the context of his goal, which is to spread Liberal Judaism, he rarely cites the sources of his ideas. We are
left with only clues and inferences to guide us in deter-
mining what these sources were. On his early life these
clues are provided by his cousin Lucy Cohen, who gathered
many of Montefiore's letters and her own reminiscences,
combining them into a book of recollections.[4] From Cohen
we learn that Montefiore's mother was a Reform Jewess who
observed the dietary laws. His father was not religious
at all but adhered to the rudiments of Judaism in defer-
ence to his wife's sensibilities. Possibly then it was
from his parents' example that Montefiore learned that
Judsiam need not be observed in the Orthodox fashion if
one desired to be a good Jew and a good human being.

The role of Montefiore's teacher and friend, Benjamin
Jowett, can be established with more assurance. Jowett,
the master of Balliol College, Oxford, when Montefiore
studied there, was the premier classicist of his day and a
Liberal Christian. In 1893 he wrote to Montefiore, "The
Jews need not renounce the religion of their fathers, but
they ought not to fall short of the highest, whether
gathered from the teachings of Jesus or from Greek philosophy."[5] Presumably then it was from Jowett that Montefiore picked up the major elements which distinguish him
from other Jewish Reformers--the necessity of working
Greek and Christian ideas into the new Judaism and the
efficacy of combining the old and the new religions. It
is also possible that Jowett's Liberal Christian theology
influenced Montefiore's belief that dogma is not as essential as ethics.

That the ideas Montefiore developed in his youth were
to have a lasting effect on his life is suggested by his
own words. For example, while at Oxford, Montefiore main-
tained a diary. In it "he foresaw...the need of a rever-
ent and sympathetic approach to biblical criticism, he
held [for] a pruning of ritual and dogma, and...for a

fuller social clarity in Jewry, the need for a fuller
social objective."[6] As will be demonstrated, these are
precisely the ideas he championed in all of his writings
and in the example of his life. The diary makes specific
reference to the Bible, but when Montefiore wrote about
the Rabbis, the very same concerns are to be seen. In
1925, at the age of 67, he wrote to Cohen that "my remarks
about Jews are really 90% of them simply childhood feelings and a little veneer....I don't think I have grown up
or changed much."[7] Thus all the evidence from Montefiore's
early life, from before he commenced his formal study of
Judaism, indicates that he had acquired preconceptions
which would color his entire career.

Montefiore began his formal study of Judaism at the
Reform seminary of Berlin, the *Hochschule für die Wissenschaft des Judentums*. Later he hired Solomon Schechter to
be his tutor in Rabbinics. It is impossible to say whether this early decision to study with Reformers and traditionalists was influential in the later decision to try to
work with traditional Jews, or whether Montefiore already
had the idea of amalgamating the two groups even before
beginning his formal studies. In either case, we once
again find in his youth a pattern which will be reflected
throughout later life. At this late date it is not possible to determine exactly what or under whom Montefiore
studied at the *Hochschule*. It appears obvious, though,
that it was at the Reform seminary that Montefiore became
deeply imbued with the tenets of the Reform Movement and
the scientific study of Judaism upon which it is based,
both of which he was to champion for the rest of his life.

A comparison between Montefiore's attitudes and those
of Schechter suggests that the student incorporated at
least some of the attitudes espoused by his teacher.[8]
Both men viewed emancipation as an attractive force,
though Montefiore was much more assimilationist than was
his teacher. Both held a deeper appreciation for Rabbinic
opinions than was currently fashionable among other

Reformers, though as noted, Montefiore placed nearly all
his emphasis on *Midrash* and *Aggadah*, while Schechter was
influenced by and practiced *Halakhah*. Both men held a
belief in the evolutionary nature of mankind's understanding of God and the Law within developing traditions,
though Montefiore believed that revelation could be found
outside the Jewish tradition, whereas Schechter did not.
Finally, both men were of the opinion that their respec-
tive branches of Judaism should be very broad so as to
encompass as many beliefs, attitudes and people as possible. While we are in no position to prove that Montefiore learned from Schechter the attitudes they share, it
is a reasonable guess that the teacher did impart his
views to his student, a guess strengthened by the knowledge that Montefiore always held Schechter and his ideas
in the highest regard.[9] In many ways, of course, the
student differed from the master. Where Schechter believed that the Jews were a unique people despite their
dispersion throughout the world, Montefiore always contended, in the spirit of the Paris Sanhedrin and the general spirit of Reform, that Jews were not a people but
citizens of the lands in which they lived. They were
bound together, if at all, only by a common religion.
Axiomatically, while Schechter supported Zionism, Montefiore continued the Reform tradition of opposing it.

This brief look at the forces which influenced Montefiore's ideas has provided the necessary preamble to his
views on religion and the Rabbis. What he likes of the
Rabbis, he keeps in the new religion; what he does not
like, he censures or ignores. In essence, then, it can be
said and will be demonstrated that when writing on the
ancient Rabbis, Montefiore was really writing on modern
Liberal Judaism.

NOTES

INTRODUCTION

[1]W. R. Matthews, *Claude Montefiore: The Man and his Thought* (Southampton, England: University of Southampton, 1956) p. 23.

[2]Montefiore's *oeuvres completes* may be found in Lucy Cohen, *Some Recollections of Claude Goldsmid Montefiore, 1858-1938* (London: Faber and Faber, Ltd., 1940) pp. 267-72.

[3]Claude G. Montefiore, *Liberal Judaism* (London: Macmillan and Co., Ltd., 1903) p. 112, announces this purpose: "Yet in spite of our differences in belief, there can still, I think, remain something of truth and value. There can still remain a view of life--it may be even clarified and enobled--which will link us with our orthodox brethren and with the historic past, and will stamp our religion with a peculiar Jewish characteristic. ...Surely if this be so, the result would add to the richness of the world."

[4]Cohen, *Recollections*.

[5]Quoted in ibid, p. 59. F. C. Burkitt was, I think, correct when he wrote in a *Festschrift* dedicated to Montefiore that Montefiore's contributions to religion and learning could not have been made without Jowett's influence (*Speculum Religiones* [Oxford: Clarendon Press, 1929] p. 1).

[6]Quoted in Cohen, *Recollections*, p. 57. The description is by a Professor Cock.

[7]Ibid., p. 135.

[8]See Norman Bentwich, *Claude Montefiore and his Tutor in Rabbinics* (Southampton, England: University of Southampton, 1966).

[9]Of his teacher, Montefiore wrote in the preface to his *Hibbert Lectures* of 1892 (*Lectures on the Origin and Growth of Religion as Illustrated by the Religion of the Ancient Hebrews* [London: Williams and Norgate, 1893] p. x) that: "To Mr. Schechter I owe more than I can adequately express here. My whole conception of the Law and of its place in Jewish religion and life is largely the fruit of his inspiration and teaching, while almost all the Rabbinic material upon which that conception rests was put before my notice and explained to me by him." These thoughts are echoed in ibid., p. 465.

CHAPTER I

THE RELIGIOUS BASIS

To Claude Montefiore ethics is religion's only
essential ingredient. Dogma and ritual are superfluous;
the miracles of the two Testaments are merely canonized
myths. The Old Testament should not be read as evidence
which substantiates the Oral Law. *Tanakh* is the work of
men who, though divinely inspired, wrote for their times,
not necessarily for ours. Modern men must retain only
that which still holds true, and disregard the rest.
None of this is strikingly original to Montefiore. All
of it had been espoused by one or another of the German
Reformers of the nineteenth century. The stress on ethics
was the universal constant amongst all the Reformers. As
Mordecai Kaplan put it, "the shift in Jewish religion of
the center of gravity from ritual observances to ethics
is at the very heart of the metamorphosis which Judaism
is undergoing."[1]

As to the Talmud, like Abraham Geiger, Montefiore is
willing to accept it as valid authority, as a jumping-off
point on the road to reform. Like Samuel Holdheim he
views the Talmud as a man-made institution, centuries long
in development, which should not be allowed to interfere
in the necessary work of Reform. On balance, Montefiore
seems a little closer to Holdheim's position as expressed
at the Brunswick Conference of 1844. There Holdheim had
argued that it was not God who gave the Rabbis authority
but the confidence of the Jewish community of the time.
Thus "anything which upon unbiased, careful criticism contradicts the religious consciousness of the present age
has no authority for us."[2] The essential difference between Montefiore and Holdheim on this point is that whereas Holdheim is more willing to abandon Talmudic elements,
Montefiore is more willing to save them if at all possible.

7

To both, however, the Rabbis are merely a human source, only some of whose corpus is of use to the modern world.

In three important ways, however, Montefiore differs from the German Reformers. All the major Reformers preached that *Halakhah* could be safely ignored. However it was left to Montefiore to argue that not only did the Law not have any salvific value in the modern world, but that it never had had any.[3] Thus Montefiore argues a position similar to the early church father Aphrahat who also claimed that Judaism's Ritual Law had never had any salvific value.[4] The second way Montefiore goes beyond the other Reformers is that he alone argues that *Aggadah* should be emphasized in an effort to show the Christian world the glorious heritage of Judaism. Indeed, at least one reason for writing *The Synoptic Gospels*[5] and *Rabbinic Literature and Gospel Teachings*[6] was to show that many of Jesus' teachings were consistent with the attitudes of those very Pharisees and Scribes who are condemned in the New Testament. In a similar vein, Montefiore wishes to demonstrate the truths of Liberal Judaism to traditionally-minded Jews and to win them over to his position. In this regard Montefiore was also willing and anxious to work with Orthodox thinkers, most notably Israel Abrahams and Herbert Loewe.[7] From these associations Montefiore apparently hoped to gain respect for his views within the Orthodox community. In return Montefiore was willing to afford traditional Jews the opportunity of countering his Liberal views with Orthodox ones of their own. This is yet another way in which Montefiore was at variance with other Reform leaders. After initial attempts to win over traditionalists, the German Reformers of the nineteenth century had abandoned their attempts at reconciliation. Montefiore never ceased his efforts to win over his opponents.

Montefiore's Writings

The source of the preceding generalizations is, of course, Montefiore's *oeuvres completes*. These can be roughly divided into scholarly and popular writings. Of the former, his very first effort demonstrates the most prodigious and sustained degree of scholarship he ever attained. *The Hibbert Lectures* of 1892, entitled *Lectures on the Origin and Growth of Religion as Illustrated by the Religion of the Ancient Hebrews*,[8] offer a masterly synthesis of then-current German Protestant Old Testament scholarship. Moreover, *The Hibbert Lectures* present Montefiore's earliest views on rabbinic theology and make evident the tremendous influence of the Prophets on him. The eighth century B.C.E., he writes here, supplies us with the first indisputably authentic and homogeneous Biblical writings. It was also the era of the four great Prophets: Amos, Hosea, Isaiah and Micah. These men are his ideal religious figures. He claims that they never spoke in a state of ecstasy or excitement and that they all preached ethical doctrines rather than demanding ceremonial sacrifice. Their God was righteous—"to them, Yahweh's moral attributes were co-extensive with his nature, so that there remained behind no non-ethical residuum."[9]

Already the youthful Montefiore is demonstrating some of the attributes which will mark his entire career. The stress on the Prophets constitutes a de-emphasis on the Mosaic Law—both that which was written in the Pentateuch and that which was codified by the Rabbis. Already ethics rather than ceremonialism is central and we see Montefiore's favoring of rational, non-mystical embodiments of God's word. The problem is with accepting Montefiore's unsubstantiated conclusion that the four Prophets never spoke in a state of ecstasy or excitement. The point is a major one for him, but whether it is true or not is a debatable one, a debate Montefiore avoids entirely. Merely to cite one example, the suffering servant of Isaiah (52:13-53:12) could easily be described as the

the product of a dreamer, one who was mystical and not
engaged in rational explanation. So even in the early
Montefiore, in a work designed to be read to the scholarly community of the day, the pattern of later life is
established. Rabbinic Judaism is (by implication) not the
only way to God; the Prophets with their (alleged) ration-
alism supply a better path. All of this may be true, but
it is based on a shaky premise at best.

The implications drawn above are fully spelled out
in the last lecture, "From Nehemiah to the Maccabees: the
Law and its Influence." Note should be taken of the fact
that in this very first work, most, if not all, of his
subsequent views on the Rabbis and Rabbinic Law are to be
found. Rabbinic particularism and overblown claims to
knowledge of the divine will are condemned, although their
moral and ethical teachings are praised.

Montefiore's other scholarly works, to one degree or
another, are anthologies. The most famous and widely con-
sulted of these is *A Rabbinic Anthology*,[10] but there are
several others. Mention has already been made of his two
studies on the Gospels, both of which consist of extended
quotations to which Montefiore appends his own commentary.
To these may be added *The Bible for Home Reading*,[11] a two-
volume synopsis with comments which is aimed at a popular
audience. Montefiore published these four anthologies as
agencies of Reform. As Judaism was an evolutionary religion,[12] its past must not be forsaken since there is too
much of value in it. However, those elements which deny
natural law and human reason have to be abandoned. He
argues that what he is doing in establishing Liberal Judaism is not unique. Judaism had always been developing.
Like the German Reformers before him, Montefiore argues
that the Rabbis had interpreted and expanded Scripture to
bring it into conformity with their own times. Occasionally this development had been beneficial, occasionally
deleterious. The Rabbinic religion,

> while based upon, and derived from the Hebrew
> Bible, is yet, in many ways, higher, purer, and
> more developed. On the other hand, in some
> respects, it falls below the finest and noblest
> portion of the Hebrew Bible, and it has a few
> infiltrations of superstitions alien to the Old
> Testament at its best.[13]

Just as the Rabbis had drawn from Scripture, Montefiore
felt free to draw from the Old and the New Testaments,
from the Rabbis, and from the ancient Greeks. This adap-
tation of the best of the ancients was in the nature of
evolutionary change. But in order to help Liberal Jews to
choose what was meritorious in the past, they had to be
given the wisdom of the ancients in convenient packages.
Before Montefiore's time such compendiums did not exist--
though Liberal Jews "unconsciously" knew of their heritage.
The problem, however, as he wrote in 1923, was that Liberal
Judaism was "not as rich as it should be and could be.
There is inadequate knowledge, and therefore inadequate
appropriation."[14] The result of these ruminations is the
series of anthologies, compendiums of ancient Jewish and
Christian beliefs.

Like his scholarly works, Montefiore's popular writings are designed to further the cause of Liberal Judaism.
Several are collected sermons which had been delivered in
his capacity as lay leader of the Jewish Religious Union.
Others are collections of extended essays, while the rest
are monographs. Although the various volumes have different subjects, many themes are the same as in the scholarly
works, to wit: The Law was not given as a piece to Moses
at Sinai; the books of the Bible were written piecemeal
over long periods of time and were then made whole by a
final redactor; Judaism had been and would continue to be
an evolving religion; the laws of science could not and
cannot be changed; God has no Chosen People; ethical mono-
theism is the final goal of Liberal Judaism; to achieve
the latter, Jews would benefit by incorporating the finer
elements of Christianity and Hellenism.

The Syncretic Nature of Liberal Judaism

The essence of Montefiore's religious belief is that
Judaism could only improve itself by a judicious selection
the finest elements of Biblical, Rabbinic and Reform Judaism, the teachings of Jesus and the Greeks, and the
lessons of science. In all except the last, what he seeks
to absorb are the ethical teachings of each, stripped of
legalistic concerns. From science Montefiore hopes to
draw truths of the natural world. These, he believes,
had never been, nor could they ever be, altered in a miraculous fashion. For instance, since science had dis-
proven the story of creation as depicted in Genesis, the
Biblical version had to be abandoned. But this was not a
regretful action: "because God is true and the source of
truth, it is scientific truth because it *is* the Truth,
which is here Divine, and not the Book of Genesis....The
truth can never be wrong; the truth can never be bad; the
truth is Divine. Similarly the Old Testament though not
Divine Law was, like science, written by divinely inspired
men."[15] This is not an idea unique to Montefiore. In the
debate between fundamentalists and scientists, Reform Jews
had no trouble aligning themselves with science. Montefiore's contribution, if any, was in presenting to the
laymen of the Liberal community the sum of modern Jewish
opinion on the question. The fact that his words on science appear in a sermon emphasizes his feeling that laymen
must absorb the truths of science as part of religion. He
does not see two roads to truth, religion or science,
rather just one--religion as modified by science, both
being the products of divinely inspired men.

From the Rabbis, who were also divinely inspired,
Montefiore hopes to extract an ethical basis for religion.
In order to do this he first divides their ideas in two.
That which deals with jurisprudence and legal technicali-
ties he eliminates in bulk both from his writings on the
Rabbis and from his grand design. Of what remains he
sifts out "the crude and the bad," leaving only those

ideas which are "religious and ethical."[16] Over and
again in his works, the stress is placed on how the Rabbis
took Scriptural ethical teachings and expanded or improved
upon them. "The virtues [Talmud] inculcates are pretty
much the same [as in Scripture], there are [however] some
fresh touches, some new emphasis, and some refinements,
delicacies and distinctions."[17] Ritual Law, however, has
no useful function. Both Biblical and Talmudic injunc-
tions had been made by men, not God. To a great extent
the Ritual Law was introduced merely to distinguish Jews
from their non-Jewish neighbors. To facilitate the separ-
ation, the Rabbis added the belief that the laws were of
divine origin and thus immutable. "For a law like 'Thou
shalt not steal' or 'Thou shalt not bear a grudge,' formed
part of the moral code of other religions as well, so that
by a false logic the distinguishing marks of Judaism
seemed to consist in those ritual and ceremonial enactments which are wholly peculiar to it."[18] The Law, once
understood in this fashion, could no longer be seen as
binding, and indeed while it had once had the social benefit of keeping the people cohesive, it never had any salvific value. Now that Jews are citizens of their diverse
nations, there is no longer any need to maintain such an
artificial barrier.

These opinions on the Rabbis are a compendium of
then-current opinions. The categories of religious and
ethical versus jurisprudence and legal technicalities seem
to be direct borrowings from Holdheim who had spoken of
the religious and ethical content of Judaism which was to
be retained and the political and national content which
was not binding on moderns. The stress on the Talmud as
an extension of *Tanakh* is based on the *Wissenschaft* movement. It is only with the attitude that the Law had never
been of salvific value that Montefiore stands alone.

In the New Testament Montefiore sees not only the
basis of a new religion, but confirmation of the beauties
of Judaism. To him Jesus was a prophet, but one who

taught nothing new about God.[19] The significance of
Jesus' ministry was in providing a new method of conduct
in relation to God. This cornerstone of Montefiore's
attitude towards Jesus is not original, but is dependent
on Foakes-Jackson and Blake[20] and G. F. Moore.[21] Some of
Christianity's "advances" on Old Testament conceptions are
the intensity and the purity of Jesus' love of God the
father and the spiritual vision of God in the Fourth Gospel. Of "the teaching of the first Epistle of John that
'God is Love'...nothing can be more striking or more
noble than the ethical use to which the doctrine is put,
or the argument which leads up to it."[22] Of equal value
to Montefiore is Christianity's view of God's relations
with man. Where Rabbinic Judaism suffers from the assumption that God is only concerned with Jews (particularism),
Christianity preaches God's universal love for all men and
the common bonds of humanity. When Paul wrote: "There
can be neither Jew nor Greek...," he expounded this principle of universalism. To Montefiore, all men are equal
under God. None is chosen as a special people. Of the
New Testament and its value to Judaism, Montefiore advocates: "Let us not then persist in keeping to a poorer
Judaism than we need. Why should we not make our religion
as rich as we can? Jesus and Paul can help us as well as
Hillel and Akiba. Let them do so. What is good in them
came also from God."[23]

With these words Montefiore seems to cut himself off
from the mainstream of Judaism, both traditional *and* Reform. The obvious question to ask is whether the incor-
poration of Christian principles is a revolutionary departure or merely just one more step in the evolutionary
principles Montefiore espouses. On one level the action
is clearly revolutionary. Nowhere else in the history of
mainstream Judaism can such an idea be found. True, the
Frankists held many beliefs in common with Christianity,
but they were hardly in the mainstream of Judaism. The
Rabbis were not loathe to condemn Christianity.[24] There

were medieval commentators who saw Christianity (and
Islam) as steps toward the true religion but this school
perceived the flow of history going in the opposite direction than Montefiore did. To them Christianity will imbue
the Gentile world with Jewish attitudes, putting Christians onto the road to the true religion, Judaism. Montefiore sees true religion as a Judaism which has adopted
elements of Christianity. The Paris Sanhedrin in effect
proclaimed that Jews and Christians worshipped the same
God, though in a different fashion, implying that each way
of worship was a valid means of communication with Him.
The Sanhedrin therefore argued that the two religions were
parallel; but parallel lines never meet. The two religions were and should be separate but equal. Abraham
Geiger, the greatest of the nineteenth century Reformers,
was deeply suspicious of any attempts to Christianize
Judaism. Even the more revolutionary Holdheim advocated
only that Jews should become assimilated to German ways.
He did not favor assimilation of Christian doctrines. In
this light then, Montefiore's argument that Jews should
adopt elements of Christianity is clearly radical.

There is, however, another way of looking at the
matter which indicates that Montefiore was more evolutionary. In antiquity, the Rabbis and even the canons of
Scripture had already Judaized Gentile ways. Daniel contains an apocalyptic vision; Purim, quite possibly, was
originally a Babylonian festival; the Rabbis frequently
resorted to Greek when no Hebrew or Aramaic words were
available to express a particular idea which was not in
the tradition (*prosbul* comes to mind immediately). Montefiore, who claims over and again to be in the footsteps of
the Rabbis, is clearly in this tradition. Additionally,
Montefiore is in the tradition of the nineteenth century
Reformers. They had advocated adopting Christian customs
--music, mixed seating, sermons in the vernacular, robes
for the Rabbis (who were even called "ministers" in the
English Reform Movement). Montefiore can thus be seen as

taking this step and merely advancing it one degree further. Not only should Jews emulate the external forms of Christianity, they should also search the tradition and extract the best that Christian ethics has to offer. Thus his suggestion that Jews adopt Christian thought is not as radical as it first seems; it is merely unique, but within both the traditional and the Reform pattern.

The same considerations are at work when Montefiore advocates appropriating the best of Greek thought. He argues that from within Hellenistic civilization too there is much which Judaism can absorb with profit. Stressing that borrowing Greek thought was not without precedent in the "Wisdom of Solomon" and in the careers of Philo and Maimonides, Montefiore argues that contemporary and future Liberal Jews are once again in an excellent position to learn from the Greeks. In the first place there are similar ideas in Greek philosophy and the Jewish Bible so that the "Greek fortifies and illumines the same thought as expressed in the Hebrew."[25] Additionally, there are Greek virtues which are unique to Hellenism and not found in the Bible. "Greek religious thought and Greek religious teaching, in some of their nobler forms and phases are not, it is contended, too remote and too unlike Jewish thought or teaching for Judaism to be able to absorb and assimilate certain elements of them to its own profit and edification."[26] Indeed, since Judaism has always been, and Liberal Judaism still is, an evolving religion, it can only profit from such acquisitions. Going one step further, Montefiore demands that "within the limits of Truth and of its own self-consistency, Liberal Judaism *must* hellenise."[27] Not to do so would be to abandon one of the two great foundation stones of Western civilization. "The great Hebrews and the great Greeks will always be of the center of Western civilization. They are the two chief roots of our civilization, and from these roots Western humanity will long, if not ever, continue to draw spiritual nurture and refreshment."[28]

Some of the *similar* developments within the Greek and Hebrew traditions include wisdom and reasonableness, the purging of superstition from religion, and concerns of spiritual purity. Hellenism was *superior* to Rabbinic Judaism in at least two respects. In the Rabbinic age, when Hellenism had been cast out and condemned, "formlessness and intemperance ruled supreme; the language tends to become poor, rambling, discursive; laws are heaped on laws without moderation or limit, and the religious ideal becomes one of number and excess and multiplication, whether in words or in ordinances, rather than of balance and order and reasonableness and gracious wisdom and seemly restraint."[29] Liberal Judaism arose in part to remedy this specific grievance.

The second case in which Hellenism was superior to Rabbinic Judaism was in its idea of divinity. "Zeus is much less purely and nationally Greek than Yahweh is Israelite. Or, rather, he is, on the one hand, identified with the head-God of many other nations; and, on the other hand, he fades into the impersonal, nameless and many named divine nature, the supreme Deity who is one and many at one and the same time, who is the soul and the law and the reason of all the universe, immanent in it, if also transcendent above it."[30]

These comments evoke several responses. Quite obviously Jews in the past, most notably Philo and Maimonides have appropriated Greek patterns of thought despite Thorlif Boman's contention that such an amalgamation is impossible.[31] To this day figures such as Mordecai Kaplan, to cite a single example, argue that the Hellenic tradition has added "a sense of reality, or reason and of the intelligence, for the fostering of which man should regard himself as morally responsible."[32] But then we come to some problems.

The contention that Rabbinic writing was formless, etc., because it lacked Greek influences is a debatable point. Indeed Montefiore himself equivocates on the

matter. The statement in question was drawn from *Liberal
Judaism and Hellenism*. In *The Old Testament and After* we
find a similar view expressed. "It is a great loss that
few Gentiles, learned in the rhetoric and poetry and philosophy of Greece and Rome became converts and Rabbis.
No real development in theology was possible without
philosophy, and no philosophy could come except from
Greece." As a result, while there may have been some
order and system and reason in the realm of ritual and
law, "religious and ethical conceptions and ideas were
under no control, were formed into no system, were allowed
to run riot."[33] But this time the statement is immediately modified. There were advantages to this lack of form,
especially in that it prevented a stiffening of doctrine
into dogma. The "scholasticism" which produced Rabbinic
Judaism was better than the scholasticism "which produced
puerilities such as those which disfigure medieval Christianity." It is worse, he argues here, to tie up thought
(as in Christianity) than merely to tie up action (as in
Rabbinism). "Whether you may wear a handkerchief on
Saturday is a childish subject for discussion; yet it is
little likely to produce heretics who are burnt alive at
the stake."[34]

This contradiction alone is enough to puzzle the
reader, and yet there is still another even more peculiar.
In *Judaism and St. Paul*[35] one of the central messages is
that diaspora Judaism in antiquity, which was affected by
Greek ways, was poorer on every count than Palestinian
Judaism which was free of Hellenistic influences. That
rather odd statement will be discussed in detail in the
following chapter, but for now it is enough to say that
Montefiore was clearly confused on the question of whether
or not Greek influences had benefited Judaism in the past.
He was, however, consistent in his admonition that Judaism
should adopt Greek philosophy in the present.

On the subject of incorporating Greek thought into
modern Judaism, what Montefiore does not say is rather

interesting. Presumably it was the eminent Jowett who
first introduced Montefiore to the necessity of bringing
Greek ideas into Judaism. Still, Montefiore had to be
cautious. The Greeks, after all, had been pagans; Chris-
tianity had become muddled through its acceptance of
Aristotle and Plato; and Montefiore does not want his
Jewish readers to reject him because of an over-zealous
endorsement of foreign (though certainly familiar) ideas.
So he is ambiguous. Never once does he suggest specific
Greek thought worthy of emulation; rather he speaks
vaguely of reason and order. He does not say that Liberal
Judaism should adopt the philosophy of the Stoic, Cynic,
Platonic or Epicurian schools. Rather, he advocates a
Greek philosophic milieu. He can then neatly skip around,
speaking of advantages and difficulties inherent in Greek
ideas, discussing the merits of some Jewish adaptations in
the past while still maintaining that not every amalgamation has been successful.

The last of the elements from which Montefiore draws
his Liberal Judaism is the most obvious of all: the Reform
Movement of the nineteenth century. From this he extracts
his ideas of order in the service, repudiation of the
Sinaitic Oral Law, notions of the universality of God, and
antagonism to Zionism and to a personal Messiah. What
distinguishes Montefiore's Liberal Judaism is the continued use of *Aggadah* and the concept that Christianity
and Hellenic/Hellenistic doctrines should be incorporated
into Judaism.

Thus far we have been looking at the component elements of Liberal Judaism. Montefiore himself summarizes
his religious belief as one which is free from the re-
straints of the past. This freedom is exercised in five
ways:

1) "It modifies or enlarges the doctrines of its
   past--the doctrines which it inherits or finds--
   so as to make them consistent with each other
   and in harmony with the highest conceptions of
   truth to which it can attain."

2) It aims at universalism and universalization
   by abandoning the purely national aspects of
   Judaism and stressing instead its religious
   elements.

3) & 4) The emphasis is on prophetic, not
   priestly, elements within Judaism. Liberal
   Judaism therefore abandons concepts of
   clean and unclean along with hopes for the
   restoration of the Temple and animal sacrifice.

5) Liberal Judaism is free to accept the results of Biblical criticism and therefore
   to reject belief in the miraculous.[36]

This sketch of the religious elements which Montefiore blends to form Liberal Judaism has been designed to
illustrate the sources of Montefiore's religion and to lay
the groundwork for a fuller study of his views on, and
uses of, the ancient Rabbis. We have seen that his movement is not simply German Reform transferred to Britain,
but a new departure. At one and the same time he keeps
much the Germans had established, extends a good deal of
it, and adds new elements as well. As to the Rabbis, his
purpose is to adapt their best qualities to the new Judaism. In the next chapter attention will focus on Montefiore's specific views on the Pharisees and on the Rabbis.
At the same time the tendentious nature of his writings
will be explored in greater depth.

NOTES

CHAPTER I

[1]Mordecai M. Kaplan, *The Greater Judaism in the Making* (New York: The Reconstructionist Press, 1960) p. 109.

[2]Quoted in David Philipson, *The Reform Movement in Judaism* (New York: The Macmillan Co., 1931) p. 145.

[3]This is a frequently made or implied assertion. See, for instance, *Outlines of Liberal Judaism* (London: Macmillan & Co., Ltd., 1912) pp. 134ff.; *The Hibbert Lectures*, pp. 478, 510. Not only had the Law never had any salvific value, but it was frequently a negative function of Judaism; see *Liberal Judaism*, pp. 94ff.

[4]See Jacob Neusner, *Aphrahat and Judaism: The Christian Jewish Argument in Fourth Century Iran* (Leiden: E. J. Brill, 1971).

[5]Claude G. Montefiore, *The Synoptic Gospels* (two volumes; New York: KTAV Publishing House, Inc., 1968).

[6]Idem, *Rabbinic Literature and Gospel Teachings* (London: Macmillan and Co., Ltd., 1930).

[7]Abrahams was Montefiore's co-editor of the *Jewish Quarterly Review* and the man to whom *Rabbinic Literature and Gospel Teachings* was dedicated "in reverence and gratitude." Loewe was co-editor of *A Rabbinic Anthology* (New York: Schocken Books, Inc., 1974) and a contributor to *Rabbinic Literature*. A fuller analysis of this latter relationship will be found in Chapter III.

[8]*The Hibbert Lectures*.

[9]Ibid., p. 122. When Montefiore was later to describe his ideal religious service, he argued that rather than placing the scrolls of the Law in the Ark, a copy of the Prophets should be given the honor of this central location; see *Liberal Judaism*, p. 125.

[10]*A Rabbinic Anthology*.

[11]Claude G. Montefiore, *The Bible for Home Reading* (two volumes; London: Macmillan and Co., Ltd., 1925).

[12]This is another frequent assertion to which whole books are devoted. For instance, *The Old Testament and*

After (London: Macmillan and Co., Ltd., 1923) and *Liberal Judaism and Hellenism and other Essays* (London: Macmillan and Co., Ltd., 1918) are made up of a series of chapters designed to show how progressive stages of Judaism were each an "advance" on what preceeded.

[13]*A Rabbinic Anthology*, p. xx.

[14]*The Old Testament and After*, p. 549.

[15]Claude G. Montefiore, *Truth in Religion and other Sermons* (London: Macmillan and Co., Ltd., 1906) p. 4.

[16]*A Rabbinic Anthology*, pp. viii, xi.

[17]*The Old Testament and After*, p. 420.

[18]*Liberal Judaism*, p. 94.

[19]Claude G. Montefiore, *Some Elements of the Religious Teachings of Jesus* (London: Macmillan and Co., Ltd., 1910) pp. 1-29.

[20]*The Beginnings of Christianity*, cited in *The Old Testament and After*, pp. 201-02, 205.

[21]*History of Religions*, cited in ibid., p. 204.

[22]*The Old Testament and After*, p. 208.

[23]Ibid., p. 291.

[24]See Robert Herford, *Christianity in Talmud and Midrash* (New York: KTAV Publishing House, Inc., 1975) pp. 35-96.

[25]*Liberal Judaism and Hellenism*, p. 187.

[26]Ibid., p. 188.

[27]Ibid. My emphasis.

[28]Ibid., p. 191.

[29]Ibid., p. 201.

[30]Ibid., p. 202.

[31]Thorleif Boman, *Hebrew Thought Compared with Greek* (New York: W. W. Norton & Company, Inc., 1970).

[32]Kaplan, *The Greater Judaism*, p. 484.

[33]*The Old Testament and After*, p. 298.

[34]Ibid., p. 299.

[35]Claude G. Montefiore, *Judaism and St. Paul* (New York: Arno Press, 1973).

[36]*The Old Testament and After*, pp. 557-58.

CHAPTER II

LIBERAL JUDAISM'S USE OF THE RABBIS

Montefiore constantly uses the Rabbis as tools to
develop, expand and explain the principles of Liberal Judaism. He argues that he is following in their footsteps
while avoiding or correcting their mistakes. Thus what he
perceives as good Rabbinic doctrines are praised and retained. The bad or the useless he avoids or cites only as
a horrible example. On balance, Montefiore consistently
tries to find advances on *Tanakh* in the ethics of Rabbinic
Aggadah and *Midrash*. These advances, he argues, are all
part of the evolution of Judaism. Problems do arise, however, when Montefiore tries to fit the Rabbis (and the
other ancients) into his modern religious system. Since
his purpose is largely apologetic, it will be noted in the
survey which follows that not infrequently Montefiore falls
into the trap of having to twist the views of the Rabbis
and those to whom they are compared in order to meet the
exigencies of specific arguments. The result of this tendency is that Montefiore's readers often learn more about
his prejudices than they do of his subjects.

Montefiore on Pharisaic Judaism

Montefiore's opinions on the Pharisees are found in
three of his works. "From Nehemiah to the Maccabees: The
Law and its Influence," the concluding chapter of *The Hibbert Lectures*, contains many of the thoughts which were to
permeate his entire career. It is also the only piece of
writing to deal exclusively with Pharisaic Judaism. The
second source is *Rabbinic Literature and Gospel Teachings*.
This extensive analysis seeks to demonstrate that much of
what Jesus taught (with particular emphasis on Matthew's
version of the Sermon on the Mount) was parallel to then-
current "Rabbinic" thought. Lastly, in *Judaism and St.*

25

Paul,[1] Montefiore makes great (though ultimately unsuc-
cessful) efforts to prove that the writings of the Apostle
do not reflect contemporary Pharisaic opinions, but rather
an inferior form of Hellenistic Judaism.

To Montefiore, Pharisaic/Rabbinic Judaism is a religion based on Law. "It began to receive this character on
the introduction of Deuteronomy; it was confirmed in it by
the reformation of Ezra; while the final triumph of legalism was brought about by the persecution of Antiochus."[2]
On one level this observation is an historical assessment
based on primary and secondary evidence. On a deeper
plane, Montefiore is informing his *fin de siècle* audience
that Orthodox Jewish claims that Moses was the author of
the Pentateuch and that he received an equally binding
Oral Law at Sinai are historically untrue. What he posits
instead is the notion that the rigid legalism of the
Pharisees resulted from attempts to Hellenize Judaism.
This persecution, then, was a catalyst, and the reaction
to it was just one more development in the evolution of
Judaism.

Somewhat later the contention that legalism was the
response of Jews to the persecutions of Antiochus is re-
peated, with the effects of the persecution, both good and
bad, more clearly spelled out:

> In calmer moments, during Persian and early
> Grecian periods, the Scribes...appear to have
> laid greater stress upon the ethical part of
> the law than upon its ritual; but when Hellenism
> [*sic*] became a danger, and still more when apos-
> tasy and persecution began, the prescription of
> clean and unclean, and all the ceremonialism
> which pertained to the individual, became of the
> utmost value and importance in accentuating the
> difference, as well as strengthening the barrier,
> between the observing subjects of the law and
> the polluted outer world of Jewish apostates and
> Gentile foes. Men died for the law's sake; and
> when all its enactments were believed to have
> issued from the same divine source, a single
> ceremonial injunction could easily be regarded
> as a type or symbol of the entire code.[3]

Montefiore's stress on the shift from ethical standards to Ritual Law indicates his disapproval. Indeed, in
describing the ritual law he had already referred to it as
a group of "puerile prescriptions" which not only "inter-
fered with social intercourse, but tended to set up a
false ideal of external sanctity."[4] The negative ramifi-
cations of this tendency are continually stressed. Since
duty, goddness, and piety were all equivalent terms for
the fulfillment of the Law, it was impossible, he argues,
to determine who the good man was. To Montefiore, such a
person is he who emphasizes spirit rather than form, "motive rather than the deed....But the legal tendency would
be precisely the opposite."[5] When he began to postulate
Liberal Judaism, Montefiore sought to correct this wrong.
What he did in effect, when delivering *The Hibbert Lectures*, was to establish the groundwork for all the reforms
of the future.

Significantly, this section, so full of the negative
aspects of the legal emphasis, ends with a redeeming quality, the glory of the Rabbinic principle of God's forgiveness:

> This simple confidence accurately represents
> the attitude of the legalist. He is not puffed
> up by the consciousness of his own fidelity; if
> he has learned a practical Torah, he claims no
> merit to himself, for 'there unto was he created.'
> His sins and inadvertances do not drive him to
> despair, for his God is gracious and full of
> compassion.[6]

Had Montefiore been a strict idealogue, confident of
the superiority of the truths preached by modern scular
Judaism, he would not have sought to salvage Rabbinic Judaism in this fashion. But it is his nature to find *advances*, to look for progress, even in those aspects of
religion with which he personally does not agree, and so
he is ever anxious to preserve something of the Rabbinic
spirit.

Other advances on the Biblical period Montefiore
assumes to have come from the Pharisaic era include the

Rabbis showing "much greater warmth in their moral teaching than the sages of the Bible or the Apocrypha. Many
illustrations could be drawn from their sayings of that
ardent religious enthusiasm--clear evidence of lofty moral
purpose and fervid willingness to self-sacrifice--which in
its highest and purest form is so characteristic a feature
in the teaching of Christ."[7] To cite some specific examples, the *lex talionis* was replaced with a monetary pay-
ment. The death penalties demanded by *Tanakh* were main-
tained but were frequently dispensed with and replaced by
imprisonment, a concept unknown in the Pentateuch. While
war still produced cruelties, torture was unheard of. In-
fanticide is never mentioned, while respect of old age,
the infirm and the helpless was unsurpassed in any other
extant civilization.[8]

Over and again in the course of the lecture, Montefiore reminds his audience that the moral precepts of the
post-exilic and Rabbinic religion were of the highest
order. Only the ceremonial element is disdained--and even
then Montefiore is quick to find a happier spirit in which
to view it. "The evidence of the Rabbinical literature
gives no real support to the view that there existed in
Judea a deep social cleavage between a *corps d'élite* of
Scribes and Pharisees who strictly obeyed the law, and a
mass of good, simple and ignorant people who, on its ceremonial side, neglected and disobeyed it." The reason for
this is that "to the great bulk of Jews the law was at
once a privilege and a pleasure."[9]

Once again there is a deliberate message to the
modern world in this attitude. One of the beauties of
Judaism, he is saying, is that there are no divisions between laymen and Rabbis. There is no anti-clericalism in
traditional Judaism because "on the whole, the good sense
of the Rabbis enabled them to see that great as might be
the study of law, practical goodness was greater still."[10]
As a result, the Rabbis "were thus compelled to turn for
their subsistence to ordinary occupations and handicrafts,"[11]

this despite the fact that intellectualism is the predominant feature of the Rabbinic religion. Because of his intellectual depth and saintly life "the learned Rabbi had ever been the subject of the deepest veneration,"[12] a veneration Montefiore shares.

However, this desire for learning and intellectual prowess was not confined to the Rabbis. "Everybody observed the law, and to be learned in its lore was the desire of rich and poor alike. Its study penetrated every class, and its practice was a spiritual bond which knit all classes to each other."[13] Only the "*Am ha-Arets*," the people of the land, out of ignorance, carelessness or independence, did not observe the Law. Montefiore assumes that this lack of observance resulted from the burdensome agrarian laws of purity. But even their objections were nullified when, after the destruction of the Temple, the enactments became obsolete and impracticable.[14] So Montefiore's message is that the Rabbis had founded a religion without caste, without oppression and without burden.

Yet with all of the advantages inherent in Pharisaic Judaism, Montefiore wishes to abandon it. The reasons for this are threefold. First, Rabbinic Judaism was only useful when Jews were being persecuted. It had bound both the people and the religion together. In his own age, religious persecution was a thing of the past (even in 1935, the age of Adolf Hitler, Montefiore wrote that he has "rejected the defeatist theory [that Anti-Semitism was perennial] and I reject it still"[15]). Consequently the Law is no longer necessary.

Secondly, the Law was based on the false assumption that both written and oral versions were given as a piece by God to Moses. Modern historical research had proven this not to be the case. The Law was man-made and therefore had *never* had any *salvific* value and could be safely abandoned. Its moral precepts should be retained, but like the agricultural laws of purity which had so offended the *Am ha-Arets*, its legalism should be allowed to wither away.

Lastly, Pharisaic Judaism, despite parallels it had
with Christianity, was only a step in the right direction.
It still lacked certain noble aspects of the Church.
Montefiore argues that "if then, Judaism be still destined
to play a prominent and fruitful part in the religious
history of the world, it may, perhaps, be that this new
stage in its development will only ensue when it has har-
moniously assimilated to itself such of the Gospel teachings as are not antagonistic, but complementary to its own
fundamental dogmas, and has freely and frankly acknowl-
edged the greatness, while maintaining the limitations,
of the illustrious Jew from whose mouth they are reported
to have come."[16]

The flattering allusion to Jesus is typical of Montefiore's attitudes. Jews could find ultimate truth about
God and human ethics only if they looked beyond the narrow
confines of *Tanakh* and the *Talmud*. Montefiore wants his
readers, both Christian and Jewish, to understand that the
truths of Jesus and the Rabbis are the same truths, though
couched in different terms and emphasizing different subjects. Thus, to Jews he teaches that Jesus was not a
wild-eyed revolutionary whose dogma was greatly at variance with what was most noble in Judaism; to Christians,
he teaches that Judaism is not an anachronistic religion.
He argues that it is demonstrable that Jesus had accepted
the true Pharisaic thoughts of his own day. This is the
message of *Rabbinic Literature and Gospel Teachings*. On
the other hand, in *Judaism and St. Paul* the opposite tendency is expounded. Paul misunderstood the glories of the
Pharisaic religion and so abandoned it.

Paul's description of himself as "a Pharisee...as to
righteousness under the law blameless" (Philippians 3:5-6),
evokes ardent disagreement from Montefiore. "Paul was no
Rabbinic [Pharisaic] Jew," but a Jew cut off from the
mainstream of Judaism.[17] In large part this statement is
based on the (faulty) presupposition that "the apocalyptic
school of thinkers or dreamers, many of whom held advanced

views about the nature of the Messiah, and all of whom
were inclined to believe that the longed-for end was at
hand" was a peculiarly diaspora phenomenon.[18] What Montefiore postulates is a greater purity of Judaism within
Palestine than without. He also assumes that this purer
Palestinian Judaism was considerably "better" than diaspora Hellenistic Judaism. To the Jews of Palestine, God
was a "simple, personable God, great and awful, but He was
also merciful and loving. He did not delegate His relations with Israel to any angel or subordinate."[19] On the
other hand, the God of Hellenistic Jews was "less inti-
mate, near and affectionate than the God of the true Rabbinic Judaism."[20]

On the question of Paul's view of the law, Montefiore
asks whether "to the Jew of the Diaspora who was disposed
to take a gloomy view of the universal domination of sin,
might not the wonder occasionally arise...how it was that
the law, given by God for Israel's welfare, had not yet
been able to destroy the evil impulse and the wicked
heart? The more commandments, the more opportunities for
transgression."[21] Here Montefiore seems merely to be pro-
jecting back onto Paul one of the Apostle's most famous
objections to the Law--Romans 7:7-8: "...if it had not
been for the law, I should not have known sin. I should
not have known what it is to covet if the law had not
said, 'you shall not covet.' But sin, finding opportunity
in the commandment, wrought in me all kinds of covetous-
ness. Apart from the law sin lies dead." Against this
view Montefiore contrasts the Rabbinic Jew to whom the Law
was "the most adorable of God's gifts, the most joyous of
the Israelite's possessions."[22]

Montefiore's conclusions about Paul are based on the
framework that 1) Palestinian and diaspora Judaism were
polar and monolithic opposites, 2) Paul did not know the
true Rabbinic Judaism (which was optimistic), and 3) the
diaspora Judaism he did know was gloomy and pessimistic--
like all other Hellenistic philosophies. It is not unlikely

that Montefiore is so anxious to disassociate Paul from
"true" Rabbinic attitudes because Montefiore clearly sees
himself in the footsteps of the Rabbis. Judaism, an
evolving religion, had seen several phases--Biblical,
Rabbinic, medieval, and most recently, Reform. All he and
his colleagues are doing is continuing the tradition. The
danger was that friends and critics alike would associate
his actions with those of Paul, an association which would
not be difficult to make, given their similarities.[23]
This explains why Montefiore (apparently alone of modern
critics of Paul) places the Apostle outside the tradition,
marking Paul as the one who did not truly understand the
beauties of the religion he abandoned, while Montefiore
remains within it, altering form and structure, but not
substance.[24]

There are two problems presented to us by these con-
tentions in *Judaism and St. Paul*. The first is that Rabbinic (Pharisaic) Judaism had no Greek strain. That argument can hardly stand the weight of evidence to the con-
trary. I and II Maccabees complain of Greek influences in
the countryside, in Jerusalem and within the Temple itself.
Despite the victory of the Hasmoneans, these were never
entirely eradicated. The author of Daniel, probably writing ca. 165 C.E., exhibits many Greek influences, not the
least of which is the apocalyptic theme which runs throughout. G. F. Moore sees aspects of this same Greek influence in the Pharisees themselves,[25] and though obviously
Montefiore cannot be held responsible for discoveries made
after his death, the Dead Sea Scrolls also contain visions
of apocalypse. The Palestinian Jesus ben Sirach, while
possibly basing his *Wisdom* on the ancient Egyptian *Maxims
of Duauf*, was clearly influenced by Greek ideas, in particular the equation of the Mosaic Law with Wisdom (24:23-
29). If Josephus' description of the Essenes in *Antiqui-
ties* 13:12 is to be believed, that sect held that Fate
governed all things--a very Greek view. Emil Schürer, who
also wrote from a distinct bias (that of a late nineteenth

century German Protestant), but who was nonetheless the finest authority of his and Montefiore's day, had previously demonstrated a tremendous Greek influence in language and culture within Palestine before and during the first century C.E.[26] In our own day, Morton Smith argues that in the period before 70 C.E., at least in the Galilee, the Greek language was predominant, possibly to the total exclusion of Hebrew.[27]

Even if we ignore the theories and discoveries made after Montefiore's death, it is still obvious that the statement that Greek influences were absent from Palestine was a tendentious one. It appears only (though often) in *Judaism and St. Paul* and, like the contention that Paul did not understand the Pharisees, it has the obvious purpose of attempting to show the Reformer Paul's mistakes and the Reformer Montefiore's correctness. Because the diaspora-raised Paul did not understand pure Judaism, he broke with it. The diaspora-raised Montefiore, however, does understand the Pharisees and the Rabbis, and only disagrees with them while remaining in their footsteps.

There is one more obvious contradiction which can be explained only if the tendentious nature of Montefiore's writings is understood. This concerns his claim that it was unfortunate that Pharisaic/Rabbinic Judaism was not influenced by Greek thought (*Liberal Judaism and Hellenism* and elsewhere) and the claim in *Judaism and St. Paul* that the "purer" Judaism of Palestine was "better" than the Hellenistic diaspora Judaism. In these two statements the distortions caused by Montefiore's apologetic purpose are quite clear. In *Liberal Judaism and Hellenism*, Montefiore is telling his readers what kind of Judaism they should develop. He is following Jowett's line. But in *Judaism and St. Paul* Montefiore's purpose is more a defense of himself and of Liberal Judaism than it is of advancing a cause. He is not like Paul who did not understand and therefore rejected Judaism; he understands it and therefore hopes to improve it.

Jesus, on the other hand, did understand Judaism and indeed was a prophet. Whenever he writes of Jesus, Montefiore seeks to demonstrate the common ground which he feels existed between the Rabbis and the founder of Christianity. But in making these comparisons, he once again falls into the trap of inconsistency. If comparisons between Rabbinic and ancient Christian doctrines are to be made, the obvious question to ask is whether the alleged parallels between the two are really parallels at all. Did the opinions of Jesus really reflect prior and contemporary Rabbinic (Pharisaic) attitudes or not? Could the Rabbis later have adopted ethical views similar to those of Jesus? In *Judaism and St. Paul* (1914) Montefiore's answer is clear. The Rabbinic opinions of the year 500 C.E. were the same as those of the year 50 C.E.[28] But in *The Synoptic Gospels* (1926) we find that "when Talmud and Gospels are compared, the originality is almost always on the side of the Gospels."[29] In *Rabbinic Literature and Gospel Teachings* (1930) a middle ground is sought: "I also assume (what I believe to be the truth) that, except in a few polemical directions, Gospel teaching had no influence upon Rabbinic teaching, and that therefore a late Rabbinic 'parallel' to a given doctrine or saying ascribed to Jesus is a true parallel in the sense that it is a true and native development or product, not borrowed from or influenced by, the Gospels."[30] While it is possible that Montefiore changed his mind twice during the sixteen-year span over which these thoughts were published, this is highly unlikely.

A more plausible reason for his inconsistency will be found in our central thesis, that all of Montefiore's works were tendentious. The first book, *Judaism and St. Paul*, is aimed at a Jewish audience and Montefiore is anxious to argue that Paul did not reflect contemporary Rabbinic attitudes. To do this he has to posit that, from the Talmud and the teachings of Jesus, one could define these Rabbinic ideas. *The Synoptic Gospels*, however, is

intended primarily to be read by the Christian community.
It is therefore more politic to ascribe chronological pri-
ority to Christian ethical doctrines which only later were
mirrored by the Rabbis. When he wrote *Rabbinic Literature
and Gospel Teachings*, Montefiore's interests were, in
large part, to demonstrate to Jews and Christians alike
that both their religions are true. Consequently, he no
longer concerns himself with the question of which teachings were more original--obviously Jesus' words were
written down first--but with the question of how close a
parallel really exists between the two. None of this is
to suggest dishonesty on Montefiore's part. Rather what
is proposed is that his mind was never made up on the
issue, leaving him the necessary latitude to argue which-
ever case best suits his perspective in a given work.

From this discussion and from the title of the book
itself, it will already have been inferred that *Rabbinic
Literature* is not exclusively concerned with the Pharisees
but that Montefiore draws heavily from statements ascribed
to later Rabbis. What he is trying to do in this book is
to emphasize the similarities between the doctrines of
Jesus and those of the Rabbis. When no parallel can be
found on the Rabbinic side, he admits it. Conversely, he
does not illustrate exceptionally good aspects of Rabbinism which were absent from or underplayed in Jesus' words.
This he would do in his studies on the Rabbis per se.

If a single theme emerges in *Rabbinic Literature* it
is that while the Rabbis taught that God was ready to for-
give the repentant sinner, the teachings of Jesus stressed
that God's love seeks out the sinner and does not wait for
his repentance. For example, Matthew 12:31-32 reads:
"Therefore I tell you, every sin and blasphemy will be
forgiven men, but the blasphemy against the Holy Spirit
will not be forgiven. And whoever says a word against the
Son of man will be forgiven; but whoever speaks against
the Holy Spirit will not be forgiven, either in this age
or in the age to come." Montefiore begins his commentary

on this by stating that "as regards severity, Jesus and
the Rabbis seem about on a par."[31]   But then he cites at
least fifteen different types of sins which to the Rabbis
could not be forgiven, only one of which has anything at
all to do with denying God.[32]   Despite this long catalogue,
Montefiore was of the opinion (which he does not directly
substantiate) that "it may be doubted whether if such a
one repented and retracted, he would not have been regarded by *these very same Rabbis* as forgiven by God."[33]

It may seem as though Montefiore's parallel is not
terribly close to the succinct teaching of Jesus as found
in Matthew. Where Matthew was brief, with only one unforgivable cause for damnation, the Rabbis listed many irrep-
arable sins but suggested ways through which repentance
might be achieved anyway, and Montefiore argues that what
was really meant was that all sins could be forgiven. The
obvious question which arises is whether Montefiore is
forcing the issue. Perhaps he saw the same problem, for
this section is closed by a note from Herbert Loewe, the
purpose of which is to show that the frameworks of Jesus
and the Rabbis, which were quite different, account for
the apparent disparities just noted.

Loewe writes that the Rabbis were in the difficult
position of having to work out a system of law as well as
administering it. Unlike Jesus, they had to be practical.
For instance, speaking as a leader in opposition, Jesus
could let off the adulterous wife without condoning adul-
tery. Had he been in power, in charge of upholding public
morality, this would not have been so easy. The Rabbis,
on the other hand, *were* in authority so they aimed at
"keeping the door open as widely as possible," while "en-
forcing respect for law and order also." They felt that
the idea of an unforgivable sin was an abhorrent one so
they "solved the problem by retaining the hypothetically
unforgivable sin and by finding excuses or extenuating
circumstances for the unforgiven sinner, so that in fact
he was forgiven."[34]   Loewe's perspective makes the parallel

clearer as well as closer. This is somewhat ironic since
it is the Orthodox and not the Liberal Jew who explains
away the difficulty. Perhaps this was Montefiore's intention. Possibly to bring traditional Jews into his fold
he allowed his friend Loewe to find the link between Jesus
and the Rabbis, a link Montefiore merely posits and which
he lets Loewe expound.

Montefiore on Rabbinic Judaism in General

The *Old Testament and After* (1923) and *A Rabbinic
Anthology* (1938) are concerned with post-Pharisaic developments. In both Montefiore comments favorably on Rabbinic ethics though in both he chides the Rabbis for
their emphasis on ritual, for their "childishness" and
for their lack of universalism. *The Old Testament and
After* deals with general thoughts and is aimed at a broader audience. The *Anthology* contains more specific statements and the tone is more scholarly.

In *The Old Testament and After* Montefiore maintains
that the Rabbinic attitudes of the year 20 C.E. were the
same as those of the year 620 C.E. There may have been a
broadening and development of doctrine, but there was also
a hardening and a fixing.[35] Thus Montefiore does not see
any great development in the Rabbis' ethical standards
(and that, after all, is all he is interested in) over the
entire period from the time of Jesus to the completion of
the Babylonian Talmud some five or six hundred years later.
This point is significant on three levels. In the first
place, by using 20 C.E. as his *terminus a quo*, he picks a
period ten years after the death of Hillel who, along with
his opponent Shammai, constituted the last of a long line
of *Zugot* (pairs), leaders of schools of conflicting
thought. The triumph of the school of Hillel could be
viewed as the period which began the homogeneity of attitude of which Montefiore speaks. By beginning with 20
C.E. he thus avoids the conflicting opinions which came
before.

In stressing this homogeneity, however, he ignores
subsequent conflicts between the Babylonian and Palestinian schools and between Rabbis within the same area. He
attempts to justify this by first acknowledging and then
dismissing the difficulty. After admitting that it would
be better to say that a particular Rabbi of a certain century held a specific view rather than to say "The Rabbis"
had such and such a view, he maintains that "yet I often
shall certainly say so, and, I believe, with adequate
justification."[36] The justifications are that the opinion
is obviously in line with general Rabbinic feelings or it
may be such a beautiful utterance that to ascribe it to
one man would be denying credit to all, or it is an anony-
mous Aggadah to begin with.[37]

The last matter once again concerns the antiquity of
Rabbinic ethics. It has already been demonstrated that
Montefiore adjusts his opinion on this question depending
on his audience. The Old Testament and After is aimed at
a Jewish audience and once again the implication is clear--
Pharisaic ethics preceded Christianity and could be deter-
mined by reading later sources. Otherwise it would be impossible to know that attitudes in 620 were the same as
they had been in 20.[38] The pattern remains consistent and
as a corollary it is not surprising to find in The Old
Testament and After an apologia for Liberal Judaism.

What hurt the Rabbis most, we are told there, was
what Montefiore called "the straitjacket of Tanakh."
Despite occasional Rabbinic efforts to explain away some
difficulties, Tanakh remained for them wholly true, divine
and good. "The crudest statements about God were somehow
not less true than the noblest; the taboo survivals--the
red cow, the waters of impurity [sic], the dietary regu-
lations--were hardly less good, and were certainly no less
divine than 'thou shalt bear no grudge, and shalt love thy
neighbor as thyself.' That is why the great move onwards
has been deferred till modern times."[39]

Indeed, Montefiore argues that it was only Liberal
Judaism which could rectify the Rabbis' mistake. The
power to view the Old Testament in its proper and true
perspective comes from Liberal Judaism's ability "to distinguish between higher and lower, good and bad, temporary
and permanent" in the Bible.[40] The Rabbis, on the con-
trary, fell into the trap of becoming "intolerant, par-
ticularist and narrow" in viewing the Gentile world, vices
which were sanctioned in the Bible and expanded, not con-
tracted, by the sages. One of the worst examples of the
entrapment by the Book was the continued anthropomorphiz-
ing of God by the Rabbis "in an unseemly and childish
manner, which could not have had effects for the good."[41]

But Montefiore was never content merely to criticize
the Rabbis. They were men who had advanced Judaism despite
their shortcomings. There were good aspects of the Rabbinic religion, good both for them and for the modern
world, which Montefiore puts into three somewhat overlap-
ping categories. First are those sayings which draw from
the Old Testament's best features. For example, the Rabbis emphasized charity, love of God, dependence on tradition, etc., features which cannot legitimately be defined
as Rabbinic and which therefore call for no further comment from Montefiore. The other two groups, refinements
of Biblical doctrines and new developments from *Tanakh*, do
however serve as springboards for discussion and explanation.

The category of new additions is much smaller. One
example is the Rabbinic emphasis on the *study* of the Law.
Tanakh, or at least the Mosaic parts of it, is concerned
with the practice and ritual involved in the Law. However,
with the destruction of the Temple and the profanation of
Jerusalem, the Law could not be observed in many of its
aspects (sacrifice, tithings, offerings, etc.). Consequently, practice was replaced by ceremonial observance
and by study, of which "the highest happiness to the
Rabbis lies in the study of the Law." In addition to the

study of the Law, observing the Law "for its own sake,"
for "love's sake," is also pleasing to the Rabbis and to
Montefiore. The Law in Rabbinic Judaism is a discipline,
a purification, a joy.

There are also new ideas about God--his nearness,
Fatherhood and immanence. The idea of the sanctification
of the Name (the acknowledgement of God's holiness through
martyrdom) is "virtually" new. "Practically" new is the
theory of the Two Inclinations (the good and evil *yetzer*).
By "practically" new it can be supposed Montefiore means
that where Genesis 6:5 and 8:21 speak of the "inclination
of man which is evil from his youth," the Rabbis added the
Yetzer Ha Tov, the good inclination, and the idea that the
bad inclination could be tamed.[42]

Still in this category of "new" developments is an
emphasis on the world to come. "Even from the point of
view of sheer happiness, it may be imcomparably better to
accept every earthly ill than to receive every earthly
good at the risk of being deprived of the eternal felici-
ties beyond the grave."[43] A clearly new conception is the
Kawwanah, the concentration of the mind, a collectedness,
a calm, an aiming towards God without which prayer is in-
effective, and which is most essential in reciting the
Shema.[44]

Most of these items called new Rabbinic conceptions
are just that. One item, however, the alleged newness of
the doctrine of the Fatherhood of God, seems to be less
than appropriate. Readers of *Tanakh* are familiar with the
Fatherhood of God as a Biblical concept. God is frequently
referred to as "Father" or "Our Father" and Israel as His
son or as children of God.[45] The only thing new, at least
according to G. F. Moore, was the concept and phraseology
of "Father in Heaven" preceded by a possessive pronoun, as
a surrogate term for God.[46] That Montefiore was familiar
with Moore's *Judaism* is clear from the many references,
all of them positive, which he made to it in the *Anthology*.
Perhaps Montefiore was just careless. Perhaps he was

looking for something complimentary to say about the
Rabbis. But neither of these explanations really rings
true. Carelessness was not one of Montefiore's faults and
Montefiore had already expressed many positive opinions
about the Rabbis.

The last category, Rabbinic refinements or extensions
of *Tanakh*, is much broader than the "new" Rabbinic additions, at least in part because it can be argued that virtually the whole of Rabbinic literature is a refinement of
Scripture. In his extended introduction to *A Rabbinic
Anthology*, Montefiore lists fourteen of these extensions.[47]
Of these the most important are:

1) The question of free will (he concludes that
   the dominant belief was that while the opportunity to do evil is there, mankind is aided
   in doing what is righteous);
2) the conception of repentance which is greatly
   developed;
3) an emphasis on justification by works (as
   opposed to faith);
4) a stress on reward and punishment as motivating factors in human behavior which has been
   abandoned by Liberal Judaism;
5) a "very strange doctrine concerning Merit
   (*Zekut*)" wherein God does kindnesses because
   of the merits of the patriarchs or the Messiah
   or the Law;
6) the "considerable advances" as regards prayer;
7) atonement and forgiveness which are also
   considerably advanced beyond similar ideas
   in the Pentateuch;
8) the doing of loving deeds as "the highest
   fulfillment of the Law and scarcely less
   precious than its study."

There are one or two points in this list which call
for some comment. One problem is the matter of stressing

rewards and punishments as motivating factors in human
behavior. This is a theme well documented in much of the
Anthology, but in *The Hibbert Lectures*, Montefiore had
consistently denied the charge that the Rabbis were eudo-
mistic.[48] Again we must face the possibility that Montefiore had changed his mind (the two books were published
forty two years apart). But a more plausible explanation
may be found in understanding the audience to which his
remarks are addressed. At least one purpose of *The Hibbert Lectures*, and certainly of the chapter on the Pharisees, is to present ancient Judaism in a better light than
had (for instance) Emil Schürer. In that cause, speaking
to Protestant clergymen and scholars, it was only natural
that Montefiore would downplay some of what he and they
perceived to be negative features of the Rabbis. *A Rabbinic Anthology* has as its audience Jewish and Christian
laymen. To such readers Montefiore could announce what
was probably his true belief--that the Rabbis did over-
stress rewards and punishments--and then append a note
that this baser side of Rabbinic Judaism has finally been
abandoned with the coming of Liberal Judaism. Once again
then, there is some evidence that Montefiore's attitudes
were influenced by his audience in an attempt to advance
a cause he felt just. Another problem with the belief
that rewards and punishments were extensions of Biblical
principles is more minor, but may merit some notice.
After a reading of Deuteronomy and other books ascribed
to "D," and after reading some of the prophets so admired
by Montefiore, it is difficult to see how the Rabbis re-
fined or altered the concept of rewards and punishment
very much at all. The blessings and curses of Deuteronomy
27 and 28, for instance, seem to carry the matter as far
as it can go.

Another matter which might be raised is on the question of the Rabbis' emphasis on works rather than faith,
an attitude Montefiore does not favor and which is associated with the whole problem of whether the Rabbis were

concerned with reason. The charge that the Rabbis placed
too much emphasis on works rather than on the character of
the individual seems clearly to be motivated by Montefiore's desire to spread Liberal Judaism. It is true that
much that the Rabbis taught was concerned with external
actions; it is also true that Montefiore's Judaism sought
to change this and emphasized salvation through the faith
of the believer instead. But in advancing this argument,
Montefiore seems merely to be setting up a straw man.
While external works may be stressed quantitatively,
Montefiore ignores the very qualitative arguments that he
discusses in the *Anthology* and elsewhere. For instance,
we have seen that in *Rabbinic Literature and Gospel Teachings* Montefiore wrote that the Rabbis believed that if one
truly repents, *any* sin would be forgiven. In the *Anthology*'s chapter on "Man's Repentance," there are over sixty
pericopes, all of which argue that God is willing to for-
give the repentant sinner. Similarly, Montefiore lists
Kawwanah, intention, as an admirable Rabbinic addition to
Judaism. Indeed he says that

> Rabbinic Judaism is a 'legal' religion but
> though the Rabbis laid enormous stress upon
> the fulfillment of the commandments, whether
> of the Written or of the Oral Law, yet they
> realized that the motive was often more impor-
> tant than the deed--even though the doing of
> a commandment as a mere duty might lead to its
> fulfillment in joy and in love, God looks to
> the intention and the purity of the deed rather
> than to its amount: to quality rather than to
> quantity.

Montefiore might also have paid greater attention to
the motives behind Johanan ben Zakkai's trilogy of major
religious concerns. The founder of the Rabbinic school
had taught that men should live as though each day were
their last. To do this the observance of three things was
necessary--Torah (the study of God's word), Commandments
(the doing of God's word) and Good deeds (service to the
Creator through service to the creatures made in His
image). Thus from the very beginning of the Rabbinic

period, the way men conducted themselves *and* the reason
for that conduct, what Montefiore calls ethics, was taught
in a religious context. Since ethics, in Montefiore's
sense of the term, is merely the motive behind good works
without which the deeds would be denied a philosophical
base, it is difficult to see what he is complaining about.
What is possible is that Montefiore's objections stem from
Protestant Christian ideas of redemption by faith alone.
Whether this is true is impossible to know, but there are
indications that Montefiore wished to model his Judaism
on the Anglican Church. Both seek as wide a doctrinal
base as possible, both are national, both are somewhat
vague on doctrinal issues, both are the products of previous reform, and both stress redemption through faith alone.

Intimately associated with this last subject of motive and deed is another point of great significance.
Throughout his writings on the Rabbis, Montefiore assumes
and argues that a distinction can be made between *Halakhah*
and theology on the one hand and *Aggadah*, *Midrash* and
ethics on the other. But whether the hard and fast distinction really exists may not be so obvious. Certainly
if one compares the *Anthology* to Solomon Schechter's *Some
Aspects of Rabbinic Theology*, an odd relationship will be
quickly noted. Montefiore claims interest only in ethics
and Schechter claims to have written his book simply "to
give a presentation of theological topics as offered by
the Rabbinic literature."[50] Yet not only is the organization of each book similar, but the same pericopes are frequently chosen to illustrate a given point--except that
what to one was ethical to the other was theological.[51]

On another level Montefiore seems to omit some funda-
mentally important questions. Perhaps they never occurred
to him, or perhaps (which is admittedly less likely in
this context), raising and answering them would not have
suited his tendentious purposes. The questions are: what
is the purpose of *Halakhah*? Is it as Montefiore believes,
simply and exclusively a collection of random pronouncements

dealing with superficial activities, designed solely to
satisfy the arbitrary decrees of God so as to win men a
place in heaven? Or might its function also be at once
more subtle and sublime, an exercise in reason? These
questions are asked neither by Montefiore nor by his con-
temporaries and so it may be unfair to impose them on him.
On the other hand, if we are concerned with how well his
views have stood the test of time, they do seem legitimate.

At least one modern critic describes the Talmud as
more than a mere legal code. According to this argument,
the Talmud's purpose is to teach submission to God's will
both through the observance of His commandments and faith
in the value of prayer.[52] The purpose of *Gemara* is to
clarify and critically examine the laws of *Mishnah* against
other related rules. The Rabbis, infatuated with reasoning, continued to discuss and give weight to the laws of
Shammai because they wanted to emphasize matters which
were in their control. By continually asking questions
even more than by offering answers, they hoped to show
how any action, however insignificant it may seem, is
really something worth asking about. Thinking, using
reason, then, was an act of piety. Similarly, the Rabbis
wished to teach the importance of the cosmic order through
their own actions.[53] This line of reasoning not only
helps us to understand that the distinction between *Halakhah* and ethics is a tenuous one, but it also effectively
refutes one of Montefiore's basic challenges to the Rabbis,
that they did not sufficiently employ reason.

It has been demonstrated in this chapter that in all
of his writings on the Rabbis, Montefiore is arguing a
case. He does this either subtly or overtly, by the in-
clusion or exclusion of pertinent materials. His case is
that Liberal Judaism is merely the latest and so far the
highest stage in the development of Judaism.[54] In order
to demonstrate this he is careful to show how Rabbinic
Judaism erred and where it was correct. He wishes to appeal to Christians and to traditional Jews, and he wants

to do it not with emotional harangues, but with reason
and the scientific study of history. However, because his
writings are tendentious, some at least of what he writes
seems to be distorted. In Chapter III, the conclusions
drawn in this section will be tested by a detailed look at
what Montefiore has to say concerning Rabbinic attitudes
on the Law and on God in his most famous book, *A Rabbinic
Anthology*.

CHAPTER II

[1]*Judaism and St. Paul.*

[2]*The Hibbert Lectures*, p. 469.

[3]Ibid., pp. 478-79.

[4]Ibid., p. 478.

[5]Ibid., p. 480.

[6]Ibid., p. 482.

[7]Ibid., p. 488. No doubt the reason the Rabbis were so favorably compared to Jesus was that Montefiore's audience, at least when these lectures were first delivered, consisted of Protestant churchmen and theologians. This is not the only time he addressed appeals to Christians. Like *The Hibbert Lectures*, *A Rabbinic Anthology* is designed in no small part to inform the great community of Liberal-minded Christians of the beauties of Judaism, and in particular of the Rabbinic aspects of the religion.

[8]*The Hibbert Lectures*, pp. 489-91.

[9]Ibid., p. 503.

[10]Ibid., p. 494.

[11]Ibid., p. 495.

[12]Ibid.

[13]Ibid., p. 497.

[14]Ibid., p. 502.

[15]Quoted in Leonard Stein, *The Balfour Declaration* (New York: Simon and Schuster, 1961) p. 176.

[16]*The Hibbert Lectures*, p. 551.

[17]*Judaism and St. Paul*, pp. 91, 93.

[18]Ibid., p. 92.

[19]Ibid., p. 26.

[20]Ibid., p. 95.

[21]Ibid., pp. 98-99.

[22]Ibid., p. 99.

[23]The similarities between Paul and Montefiore include their both being Reformers of Judaism who claimed great familiarity with the Law, who saw truth in the teachings of Jesus, and who were products of and propagated their ideas in, the diaspora, to Jews *and* Gentiles.

[24]Where Paul was pessimistic, Montefiore (as were the Palestinian Rabbis) was optimistic. While both saw virtue in the teachings of Jesus, to Paul "Christianity is not the Law *plus* Jesus Christ, it is Jesus Christ alone" (*Judaism and St. Paul*, p. 129), whereas to Montefiore true Judaism should consist of some of the Law and some of the teaching of Jesus. Truth, Montefiore argued, is found equally in both traditions despite the protestations of Orthodox Jews and Orthodox Christians. "The saints of neither religion believe in the possibility of sainthood in the other. In Abraham's bosom each would be surprised to meet the other. But God, who is above and beyond these human institutions, is not surprised at all" (p. 129).

[25]G. F. Moore, *Judaism in the First Centuries of the Christian Era: The Age of the Tannaim* III (Cambridge, MA: Harvard University Press, 1927, 1930) p. 18.

[26]Emil Schürer, *The Jewish People in the Time of Jesus Christ* (New York: Charles Scribner's Sons, 1898) pp. 24-51.

[27]Oral comments made at the Second Max Richter Conversation, Brown University, Providence, Rhode Island, July, 1976.

[28]*Judaism and St. Paul*, p. 87.

[29]*The Synoptic Gospels*, p. cxli.

[30]*Rabbinic Literature and Gospel Teachings*, p. xvii.

[31]Discussion surrounding Matthew 12:31-32 and the Rabbinic parallels is in ibid., pp. 244-46.

[32]Among these unforgivable sins are the denial of the divinity of the Law, of God or of Judaism. To these R. Nathan in the *Aboth* added five categories of people for whom there could not be forgiveness--those who sin repeatedly, those who sin in a pious generation, those who sin with the intention of repenting and those who profane the name of God. However *Yoma* 86 says that those who profane God's name and then repent and observe Yom Kippur "only leave the question in suspense; but death atones."

There are other contradictions as well. In *Yoma* 86b one
Rabbi says that God forgives a man who commits the same
sin three times, but not the fourth. "Nevertheless, in
other places we hear that the gates of repentance are
never closed." Even King Menassah repented and was forgiven. And still Montefiore finds other classes of unforgivable sins. The eleventh section of *Mishnah Sanhedrin* says the following have no share in the life to
come: those who say the Torah does not teach the resurrection of the dead, those who deny that the Torah is from
God, and Epicurus ("probably the Atheist, the Denier of
God, the Arch Heretic"). To these R. Akiba added those
who read external books and those who say the tetragram-
maton aloud. The *Gemara* further expanded the list by
giving examples of how one might deny the Law or act as
Epicurus, etc. As an afterthought, Montefiore then gives
one last example of an unforgivable sin, a different sort
of offense in that it is "ethical" not "religious" at its
base--"putting a fellow-man to shame openly." This list
is drawn from *Rabbinic Literature and Gospel Teachings*, pp.
245-46.

[33]Ibid., p. 246. In several places in his narrative
works, Montefiore makes the same point. For example, in
Outlines of Liberal Judaism (London: Macmillan and Co.,
Ltd., 1912) p. 142, he argues that after death sinners are
educated and then eventually rewarded. Hell is not possible since God has infinite mercy. It would therefore
seem as though Montefiore is imposing his own rationalis-
tic ideas back onto the Rabbis who apparently did believe
that some sins could never be forgiven.

[34]Loewe's comments are in *Rabbinic Literature and
Gospel Teachings*, pp. 246-47.

[35]*The Old Testament and After*, p. 294.

[36]Ibid., p. 295.

[37]Ibid., pp. 295-97.

[38]It should be pointed out that in *A Rabbinic Anthology* Montefiore uses virtually the same fact we are discussing here but in a very modified fashion. On p. xiv he
tells us that "there was far less change and variety as
regards the Rabbis between (say) A. D. 100 and 500 than in
England between 1500 and 1900." In the *Anthology*, a book
designed for a mixed audience, Montefiore once again
skirts the issue of the antiquity of Rabbinic ethics by
using as his starting point a period after the last Gospel
(John) had been written. Here too, then, the same pattern
emerges. Montefiore chooses or interprets sensitive facts
to suit his intended audience.

[39]*The Old Testament and After*, p. 299.

[40]Ibid.

[41]Ibid., p. 300.

[42]*A Rabbinic Anthology*, p. xxv.

[43]Ibid., p. xli.

[44]Ibid., pp. xxv, 272ff., 346.

[45]See, for instance, Exodus 4:24; Deuteronomy 14:11, 32:16; Hosea 11:1, Jeremiah 3:19; Isaiah 1:2, 45:11, 63:16, 64:8--a list which is not exhaustive by any means.

[46]Moore, *Judaism in the First Centuries* II, pp. 204ff.

[47]*A Rabbinic Anthology*, pp. xxxiv-liii.

[48]*The Hibbert Lectures*, pp. 533ff.

[49]*A Rabbinic Anthology*, p. 272.

[50]Solomon Schechter, *Some Aspects of Rabbinic Theology* (New York: The Macmillan Co., 1910) p. viii.

[51]As to organization, they both work from God to man to the Law to sin, and end with the hereafter (Montefiore) and Repentance (Schechter).

[52]Jacob Neusner, *Invitation to the Talmud* (New York: Harper and Row, Publishers, 1973) pp. xii-xiii.

[53]Ibid., pp. 125-26.

[54]In *The Old Testament and After*, p. 550, Montefiore admits that the Liberal Judaism of 2123 (200 years after his writing) would be a very different religion from the one he was then fashioning, though whether it would be better or worse, he could not say.

CHAPTER III

TEST SUBJECTS: ON THE LAW AND GOD

Rabbinic conceptions of the Law and God are the subjects which most fascinate Claude Montefiore. They are
the only topics to which he devotes space in all of his
discussions on the Rabbis and on Liberal Judaism. This is
only natural. To practice Judaism one must at least have
an idea of what the religion's conceptions of God were and
are. How have these conceptions changed? What has remained static? Should Liberal Jews continue to view God
as the ancients had? These are the kinds of questions
Montefiore addresses when he writes about God and Liberal
Judaism's perceptions of Him. As a rule, Montefiore is
comfortable with the concept that God is a unity, that He
is pure spirit, that He cares for all the creatures He has
created. When the Rabbis express similar views they are
praised and Liberal Jews are urged to follow their example.
But when the Rabbis anthropomorphize, when they say that
God loves Israel more than other people, that He wants and
needs animal sacrifice, Montefiore is quick to inform his
readers that such doctrines are anachronisms in the modern
world. If one were to balance Montefiore's qualitative
and quantitative agreements with the Rabbis against his
dissenting opinions, it would be found that by far the
heavier emphasis is with the former. As to the Law, to
the Rabbis it may have been the very breath of their nostrils, but to Montefiore it is almost utterly useless and
has always been so, except as a cement to bind the people
together in eras of persecutions. Now that Jews are not a
unique people, now that persecution is a thing of the past,
the Law, except when it has an ethical basis or teaches an
ethical lesson should and (perhaps) must be abandoned.

Because Montefiore's comments on the Law and God are
so crucial in understanding him, these enormous topics

will provide excellent tests of the assertions made in
this study. These assertions are that the consistent
purpose of all of Montefiore's scholarly and popular writings is to spread the doctrines of Liberal Judaism which,
as he devised it, is an evolving and syncretistic religion; that while there was much in Rabbinic literature
which he held in low esteem, Montefiore felt that a great
deal of it was highly admirable; that his emphasis was on
what he liked, not disliked, and that this was accomplished
by a judicious selection of what he termed the "advances
of Rabbinic Literature" (as opposed to Rabbinic Law).

A Rabbinic Anthology

In order to narrow the focus considerably, attention
in this chapter will be directed exclusively to *A Rabbinic
Anthology*. Isolating this one source has several advantages. While much of what Montefiore wrote in his earlier
books is included in the *Anthology*, as his last effort, it
provides a look at his thought in its fullest flower and
as a summation of his life's work. In addition, since it
is co-edited with Herbert Loewe, it provides an excellent
example of how and why Montefiore worked with traditional
Jews. Finally, as the *Anthology* is his most famous and
possibly most enduring effort, it does deserve special
attention.

Why the book was written at all poses an initial
problem. *A Rabbinic Anthology* is hardly unique. Already
in 1910 Solomon Schechter's *Some Aspects of Rabbinic
Theology*[1] had appeared, and in 1927, G. F. Moore had published *Judaism in the First Centuries of the Christian
Era: The Age of the Tannaim*.[2] In addition, A. Cohen's
Everyman's Talmud,[3] in Montefiore's own words, "covers in
a much more systematic and complete form than my own book,
much of the same ground."[4] Why then bring forth yet
another book on a subject so well covered by others? The
answer is suggested in another comment Montefiore makes
comparing his anthology to Cohen's: "In fact, Dr. Cohen's

book is much less subjective and impressionist."[5] While
nowhere else suggested, these words do imply that Montefiore himself saw his work as a less than objective effort. The inference then is that the *Anthology* is at
least as much an agent of Reform as his other writings.
Moore had written from a Christian perspective, emphasizing an early period, Schechter as a Conservative Jew,
stressing theology. *A Rabbinic Anthology* is designed
largely to explain Liberal Judaism's approach to the
Rabbis, to spread its doctrines and to show how it drew
from Judaism's past.

A second problem is that while Montefiore had a great
deal to gain from the association with Loewe, it is not as
immediately evident what Loewe would stand to gain from
the collaboration with Montefiore. From Montefiore's perspective, his co-editor brought along enormous knowledge
and erudition. More importantly, the partnership demonstrated that a Liberal and an Orthodox Jew could find a
via media through which schism could be avoided and the
possibility of amalgamation increased. As noted, Montefiore, at least, seems to be aiming at a Judaism based on
reason which could be as theologically all-encompassing as
the Anglican Church itself.

As for Loewe, factors of personal fondness aside, it
is at least superficially surprising to find the more traditional Jew helping to spread Montefiore's Liberal doctrine. What made the partnership possible may be found in
Loewe's own description of himself as "an Orthodox Jew...
but not a fundamentalist."[6] By this he meant that he observed the Law but was willing to allow redaction and form
criticism, etc., to teach him how the Law was devised. As
a result he believed that within the Old Testament the
seeds of the ethical foundations of Rabbinic theology were
to be found. In addition (at least according to his son),
Loewe's experiences as a teacher at Oxford and Cambridge
had taught him that students who came from homes where the
Orthodox-Liberal schism was hotly debated would, at the

common ground provided by University, apply their intel-
lects in an attempt to resolve Judaism's internal divisions.[7] All of these attitudes, of course, were matched
by Montefiore's ideas. Judaism was evolutionary, and
reason and reasonableness should be Jews' guiding lights
in their understanding of religion and God. Loewe's co-
operation might also have been spurred by a desire on his
part to retain traditional input as a counterbalance to
the Liberal ideas of Montefiore. Loewe did reserve for
himself the prerogative of casting dissenting opinions,[8]
though there *was* agreement between the two men even at
the most unusual junctures.

For example, despite the fact that Montefiore could
claim that *Halakhic* questions of purity, clean and unclean,
etc., were obsolete[9] while Loewe argued that God's Law
could never be antiquated, common ground on this vital issue did exist. Loewe argues that God had given men reason
as well as Torah: "Without reason, man cannot appreciate
Torah. Without Torah man cannot use his reason rightly."
Thus reason and Torah are inseparable and mutually complementary.[11] Hence, like Montefiore, Loewe saw an evolutionary Judaism. "If Judaism had always remained static
and incapable of moulding new conditions to old institutions as to maintain stability and renew vitality, how
poor should we have been."[12]

Loewe lists as advances the replacement of the syna-
gogue for the Temple, prayers for sacrifices, consecrated
wedlock for legalized cohabitation, and Hillel's legal
fiction of the *prosbul* for the Deuteronomic injunction
against collecting debts in sabbatical years. All of
these are significant Rabbinic advances illustrating the
evolutionary principle of God's Revelation through history.[13] Thus despite heated disagreements which do appear
in the pages of the *Anthology*, Montefiore and Loewe do
share common ground--particularly once the decision had
been reached (presumably by Montefiore) to ignore as much
as possible of Rabbinic Law (as opposed to Rabbinic attitudes towards the Law).[14]

On the Law

Montefiore's first specific reference to the Law in
his lengthy Introduction is a negative one. While to the
Rabbis the Law was the most important aspect of their
religion, the very "breath of their nostrils...yet to most
of us, it has become distant and obsolete...a waste of
mental energy and of time." If most of it were lost,
archeology, comparative jurisprudence, etc., would be
poorer "but our modern religious life would hardly be
affected."[15] Perhaps as bad from Montefiore's perspective
was its lack of literary merit--"it is without form or
artistry," and yet it had imposed itself on the masses of
Jews for thousands of years.

However, just as we will see that Montefiore is not
universally happy with every Rabbinic conception about
God, he is not completely unhappy about their attitudes
towards the Law. While the Rabbis hardened some of the
imperfections and crudities of *Tanakh*, such as God's fa-
voritism for Israel and "the doctrine of tit for tat" [*sic*],
their idea of Law was often an advance on that of the Old
Testament. "The legalism and ceremonialism of the Rabbis
are in some respects far better than the legalism and
ceremonialism of the Pentateuch; they are less priestly,
less primitive, freer from superstitions."[16]

More direct praise is found in the last words of his
Introduction, quite possibly the last words Montefiore
ever wrote for publication. This is an appeal to Christians, imploring them to understand that Redemption and
Law are not mutually exclusive. Beginning as he frequently does by objectively giving the opposing point of
view, Montefiore allows the argument that logically speaking, in a religion of Law, God has to reward or punish
according to a man's fulfillment or violation of the com-
mands of an external code. Therefore, only the possibility of happiness in heaven or torment in hell could dic-
tate men's life styles. A religion of redemption, on the
other hand, gives inward peace and joy. But, he argues,

in the 1900 years of "the greatest of the religions of redemption," hell has always been a greater reality to its adherents than in Judaism, the religion of Law. Conversely, not only did the religion of redemption wind up finding hell, but the religion of Law 'found' God no less often or less vividly than the Fathers."[17] In persecution and sorrow the Law has been a source of gladness and power.

Montefiore's purpose in writing this address to Christians is clear. His aim is not to convert them, but to show them the beauties, "the flowers," of Judaism and to disabuse them of the notion that truth resides in a single creed. In effect, he is reversing the thrust of so many of his previous arguments. Not only could Jews learn from Christianity, but Christians could still learn from Judaism. He chooses the Law as the agent of that instruction based on presumed Christian prejudices "which still linger here and there, even in England" that Judaism consisted solely of the Law.[18] So to Christians he writes that the Law brought forth goodness. At the same time he knows that Jews would read these words also and to them he has another message. The Law had been beneficial once, but it was only one aspect of Judaism, an aspect which can be safely dismissed now that its ancient and medieval function as "protection" against persecution has been superseded.

Thus far we have been looking at Montefiore's Introduction. In it are found his general attitudes on the Rabbis. Prefacing nearly each Rabbinic pericope or group of pericopes is an introductory note. These glosses can be divided into five categories--those which are simple, factual statements of what is to follow; those in which Montefiore gives a Rabbinic opinion with which he clearly disagrees but does not tell us so; those where he cites a Rabbinic opinion with which he is in agreement but does not tell us directly; those which he calls "curious," or "strange"; and those which directly reveal that the tendentious nature of the book is not limited to the Introduction, but finds its way into the core of the work itself.

The first category of notes is by far the largest,
indicating Montefiore's basic honesty. The second category, often difficult to distinguish or separate from the
first, but qualitatively different, also illustrates
Montefiore's basic approach. For instance, it is clear
from reading his narrative works that he disagrees strongly with the Rabbinic opinions he describes below, but he
does not stoop to appending pejorative comments:

1) The Israelites are fair and acceptable to God,
   only when they fulfill the commandments of
   the Law.[19]

2) The Law gives life, above all, life in the
   world to come.[20]

3) The Law's enactments must be, in one sense,
   not an obligation, in another sense, they
   must be performed, just because you are
   bidden to fulfill them.[21]

4) All the words of the Law are sweet and
   delightful.[22]

The third category is the reverse of the preceding
one. Just as Montefiore is careful to include Rabbinic
attitudes with which he disagrees, he fills the chapter on
Law with pericopes and comments favoring his own point of
view. This is necessary since he always holds that there
is much good in Rabbinic literature, good which Liberal
Judaism should maintain. To wit:

1) The Rabbis were well aware that both goodness
   and sin need not necessarily consist of
   actual deeds. To help others to virtue is
   even better than to do virtuous deeds oneself. To cause others to sin is worse than
   to sin oneself.[23]

2) But the Law should be loved and studied for
   its own sake, and not for its rewards. No
   worldly use must be made of it.[24]

3) There is perhaps an occasional perception
   that revelation is progressive.[25]

4) A prophet may even order the violation of
   a Law, if the exigencies of the moment
   demand it.[26]

In an intermediary category between the neutral comments and the tendentious ones, the words "strange" or "curious" are used. Presumably Montefiore is in disagreement with, or at least is baffled by, what he reports. For example:

1) The idea that 'fire' is made use of in the world to come is very strange. It might, on the one hand, indicate a belief in a very material heaven. Or, possibly, the world of the resurrection may still be conceived of as earth, but a finer earth than now. Or, fire may be regarded as a metaphor of God, 'the consuming fire,' or a reminiscence of the fire at the lawgiving on Sinai.[27]

2) There are strange passages in the Rabbinic literature which speak of God himself as a student and teacher of the Law. But if we remember that, to the Rabbis, Torah meant and included all wisdom, the strangeness is lessened. Perfect wisdom must, as it were, think wisdom, even as to Aristotle, God, the thinker, thinks thought. Besides being a student, God is also a teacher, of the Law.[28]

The last annotation is revealing in two ways. While Montefiore is always bothered by anthropomorphism, this passage, where God is placed in a subordinate role (to the Law?), really seems to astound him. The second point, which also serves as a bridge to the last of the five categories, is the equation between the Rabbis and Aristotle. It has already been sufficiently demonstrated that Montefiore sees a basic compatibility between Hellenic, Hellenistic and Rabbinic attitudes, and that he urges Liberal Jews to study Greek philosophy and to incorporate some of its principles into Judaism. In this annotation, while a direct plea is absent, it can only be assumed that Montefiore wishes his readers to draw the obvious conclusion that they should not be parochial in their studies.[29]

The last category, which more than any other is illustrative of the *Anthology* as an agent of Reform, is the most important. The three examples cited immediately below all reflect Montefiore's opinion that the Talmud (in its

broadest sense) was not given at Sinai, but developed
centuries later.

> 1) The Rabbis took the verse 'I hate them that
> are of a double mind.' They concluded that
> David meant 'there are they who ponder over
> the fear of God because of their sufferings,
> but not from love....An earthly ruler pub-
> lishes his decrees, and all obey them, but
> though they obey them, they do so out of
> fear only; but I am not so; from love of the
> Law I fulfill the Law.' [Montefiore says:]
> We might feel that if David had said that,
> he would have been very self-righteous. But
> we must remember that it is not David who is
> really speaking; it is the Rabbis who use
> him for the purpose of putting forth their
> ideals of morality and religion.[30]

The following expands this idea:

> 2) The Rabbis knew well enough that many of the
> enactments of the Law were the subject of
> Gentile ridicule. The law of circumcision,
> for example, which to them was so precious
> and divine (they knew nothing of its true
> origin, or of its wide diffusion among many
> savage races, and they believed implicitly
> in the account of its origin as given in
> Genesis), was laughed at by cultivated
> Hellenists and Romans. The same was the
> case with many other enactments, some of
> which, even to the Rabbis themselves, may
> have seemed (like the law of the Red Cow)
> to bear a resemblance to the customs of
> the heathen. They, therefore, *invented the
> theory* that certain ceremonial enactments
> of the Law were just arbitrary rules of God,
> which the Israelites must obey without
> criticism.[31]

There are several items of interest in this passage. That
the Rabbis were forced to invent a theory is the most obvious. Attention should also be paid to the discussion on
circumcision. It is not, Montefiore is saying, a unique
covenant between God and Abraham and through him all Israel, but a tribal relic, the origins of which are unknown, the singularity of which is non-existent. The belief in the uniqueness of the covenant illustrates the
naivety of the Rabbis who, in an equally naive way, saw
the Bible as a divine product. Lastly, the contention

that even the Rabbis may have seen a resemblance between
some of Judaism's precious laws and heathen ways seems to
be an unjust imputation to the Rabbis of Montefiore's own
twentieth century rationalisms.

This indirect argument that the Law was man-made is
pushed still further:

> 3) Contact with Christians, and the arguments
> of those who accepted the teaching of Paul,
> made the Rabbis cling the more devotedly
> to the Law. It was immutable: it was given
> as a whole: no new Law or new Covenant was
> to follow it.[32]

In this gloss we can see a return to an earlier
theme expressed most fully in *The Hibbert Lectures*. There
the contention had been made that "the final triumph of
legalism was brought about by the persecutions of Antiochus,"[33] that the Law arose as a result of persecution in
an attempt to solidify and unify the community. Here we
are told that the Law already existed in the Common Era
but that the challenge of Christianity made the Rabbis
cling to it with even greater intensity. The suggestion
is possibly that observance or evolution of the Law had
been on the wane or that *Mishnah* at least was expanded
(or invented) in response to an external threat. Either
reading extends Montefiore's argument that the Law was
man-made, and that therefore men could abandon it.

On God

Concerning Rabbinic views of God, Montefiore tells us
a great deal more than he does about their views on Law.
No doubt this is because he *agrees* more with their attitudes on the deity than he does with the Law or Rabbinic
attitudes towards it. As his purpose is to show the
flowers and not the weeds, this unequal distribution of
attention is only to be expected. It might also be suggested that since the *Anthology* had a proselytizing sub-
structure, factors enhancing this aim are to be found.
To his Christian readers, Montefiore defends the unitary

concept of God and disabuses them of the assumed belief
that the Jewish God was interested only in law, justice,
and authority, as opposed to mercy, forgiveness and charity. Since Montefiore's Liberal Judaism encompasses traditional elements, he informs Liberal Jews of those Rabbinic
conceptions of God which they too should hold and those
they should abandon. Similarly, Orthodox Jews are shown
that Liberals do not diverge greatly in their views of God
from traditional opinion but that some traditional (Rabbinic) constructs do not hold up to the light of reason
and ought therefore to be abandoned.

The clearest demonstration of Montefiore's desire to
show the Rabbis in a favorable light is the fact that he
generally balances his negative assessments with a positive aspect of their thought. In discussing Rabbinic
views on God, this pattern remains consistent. For example, his negative comments concern: a) Rabbinic propen-
sities to childishly anthropomorphize and anthropopathize
God, b) their belief that God is more loving of Jews than
of Gentiles, c) their view that some of His decrees may be
arbitrary, d) their image of God as constantly meting out
rewards and punishments for blessings and sins great and
small. On the other hand, Montefiore writes that the
Rabbinic conception of God was purer and cleaner than
Christianity's; he praises the Rabbinic notion that God
is good to all men and that His nearness, fatherhood and
immanence as manifested in the *Shechinah* was stressed by
the Rabbis.

What seems to have bothered Montefiore most, probably
because it appealed to his reason least, was the humaniz-
ing of God. To Montefiore, God was pure spirit; to the
Rabbis, He was the perfect Rabbi, loving and studying the
Law exactly as they did.[34] This, as we are told no less
than three times on a single page, is a childish conception.[35] The problem is that even if the human qualities
of God are mere metaphor, speaking about God in this
fashion and having God speak, having Him love what the

Rabbis loved and hate what they hated, affects the whole
conception of God. The Rabbis became overly familiar with
Him, and so He became less divine and more human. To
Moderns (Liberals), God may not be as vividly realized, He
may be less certain in people's minds, but He is more
divine.

These negative views are countered, however, by positive Rabbinic constructs. To the Rabbis God is near and
everywhere through the agency of the *Shechinah*. This concept is a denial of anthropomorphism, as was the scrupu-
lous observance of the Second Commandment, which prevented
Jews from graphically picturing their God. Christianity,
on the otherhand, had fallen into this trap, a trap made
easier by the human nature of the second figure of the
Godhead.

The Rabbis erred when they taught that God was more
loving to Jews than to Gentiles, a situation Montefiore
admits "frankly though sadly."[36] The presumption was that
just as the Rabbis "could honestly think that God liked,
or at least ordered, Israelites to worship Him by holo-
causts of bleeding animals, so they could honestly think
that He liked to, or, at least, would, send Gentiles *en
masse* to hell, or, at any rate, deprive them of the glorious world to come."[37] But this view too is modified--"The
Rabbis were convinced that all men were God's creatures.
'The Lord is good to all,' says the Psalmist, and the
Rabbis would heartily subscribe to the doctrine, and even
include the animals."[38]

The Rabbis were wrong when they wrote that God had a
particular empathy with Israel. To them Israel's joy was
His joy; its sorrow, its afflictions, were His too. "In
fact, it would appear that seven-eighths of God's time is
taken up by Israel, looking after them, correcting them,
grieving for them...and so on. The world was created for
Israel's sake...."[39] On the other hand, God to the Rabbis
was always God of the Universe. In the same vein, a Jew
could not sin with impunity knowing that God was on his

side--"in fact, we may be sure that such an idea, if the
Rabbis had heard of it, would have been strongly reproved
by them and repudiated."[40]

One last example of a negative view modified by a
more positive one concerns the question of rewards and
punishments. According to Montefiore there were three
"ugly" Rabbinic doctrines on the question. Bad tidings as
direct punishments from God for specific sins is the most
obvious. The second is that the righteous may be punished
heavily here so that they might be "more fully and uninterruptedly rewarded beyond the grave." Lastly, the
wicked may be rewarded here for their righteous deeds in
order that they may be more uninterruptedly and thoroughly
punished after their death.[41] But Montefiore then ends
his comments by telling us that Rabbis were blessed with a
pleasant inconsistency, the conception that "God rewards
gratis." God's forgiveness has nothing to do with our
works because mankind has no claim on God--we must love
him purely and not for any reward.[42] Montefiore's concluding words on this apparent dichotomy can also serve as
a summation of the way he viewed Rabbinic perspectives on
God in the Introduction to the *Anthology*: "So, if the
Rabbis go beyond the Hebrew Bible in *one* direction for
evil, they also go far beyond it in the other direction
for good."[43]

Just as the one chapter on Law contains various
prefatory remarks on Rabbinic attitudes, so it is with
the various chapters on God. The major difference is that
in these chapters the tendentious quality of the work is
much more in evidence. Nearly absent are the second and
third categories, those in which Montefiore agrees or disagrees with a Rabbinic attitude without telling his readers his opinions. Rather we are given, one after another,
statements indicative of Montefiore's position on specific
issues. Below are some examples:

1) I have not come across any passage which
seriously tackles the Christian conception
of the Trinity, or which attempts to show

> that a Unity, which is a simple and pure
> Unity, is a higher or truer conception of
> the divine nature than a Unity of a Trinity,
> or than a Trinity in a Unity....In other
> words, the doctrine of the Trinity (if that
> is referred to) is construed to mean Tri-
> theism, which indeed was, and perhaps still
> is, its vulgar corruption.[44]

This is one of several defenses of Christianity scattered
throughout the *Anthology* and Montefiore's works in general.
It is unique, however, in that it seems to be the only
time where he specifically takes exception to Jewish views
of the Christian conception of God. By calling Rabbinic
views vulgar in thinking that Christians believe in three
gods, he neatly skirts the question of what he himself
made of the concept of the Trinity. At best we can only
draw conclusions based on negative evidence--it is not a
form of tritheism, but neither is it the purer and simpler
view of Judaism. He thus appears to hold a middle ground.
Christians are monotheists but their dogma about God is
less rational than Jewry's.

> 2) For the Rabbis grieved over the fallen Sanc-
>   tuary. Some of them had seen it still unin-
>   jured; they had witnessed the sacrifices and,
>   inexplicable as it is to us, had felt no
>   disgust, but only joy, in all the blood and
>   the killings of goat and sheep and bull.
>   They took all that is said in the O. T. at
>   its face value; God *did* "dwell" in the
>   Temple. It *was* His earthly "house." In
>   some true, if mysterious sense, He actually
>   *was* within the Holy of Holies. For all this
>   conception, the doctrine of the *Shechinah*
>   was of great assistance.[45]

This gloss begins with Montefiore's frequent technique of
simply describing a Rabbinic attitude, but it then quickly
changes, underlining his antipathy with what he considers
a barbarous practice. Liberal Judaism has abandoned any
desire to re-establish the Temple and with it the sacrifice of animals. It views Jews as citizens of their re-
spective nations who should not forswear their homelands
and nationalities, and it considers sacrifice and Rabbinic

aspirations for a return of the practice as throwbacks to a dark age of human development.[46]

The other ingredient in Montefiore's comment is the way he discusses the *Shechinah*. We have already noted that he sees this as an advance made by the Rabbis on Old Testament ideas. Though it is based on Biblical passages, most notably Psalm 139, Montefiore views it as a unique addition to our understanding of God. But the context of the remark makes it clear that Montefiore is here preaching that the Rabbis *made up* convenient (though nevertheless occasionally admirable) doctrines as they went along to deal with problems presented to them in Scripture. The Rabbis, he tells us, were faced with more than one view of God in *Tanakh* and as a result they "were in the painful position of having to accept both sets of passages as equally true. So they tried, more or less successfully, to invent some theory which would *partially* at any rate relieve the inconsistency, and make of the discordant a harmony."[47] The key word here is "invent," for to Montefiore, that is all the Rabbis ever did—invent a legal and ethical second Law. The *Shechinah* was one of their nobler inventions. Others, such as the following, were less so:

3) The Rabbis were not averse to using the most daring, and to our taste, the most unsuitable, anthropomorphisms about God, more particularly in dealing with the relations of God to Israel or to the Law or to Moses.[48]

4) The great attributes of God are, to the Rabbis, what I have mentioned: in other words, they are the great attributes of the highest teachings of the O. T. But the particularism of the Rabbis usually prevented them (even as it prevented the writers of the O. T.) from realizing that when God, for example, delivers the Israelites by the ruin and slaughter of their foes, there is any difficulty in regarding such a deliverance as anything more than a single example of God's goodness, mercy or compassion.[49]

5) The legends with which *Esther R.* enlarges and fills out the biblical text are not entirely pleasant reading. However, much of the

> circumstances of the time in which they were
> written may explain them, there is too much
> unqualified delight in the downfall and
> punishment of Haman, and also in the awful
> revenge of the Jews upon their enemies. No
> nation is near to God except Israel. All
> other peoples but Israel are foreign unto
> God....These bizarre theories were doubtless
> themselves invented partly by national pride
> and national exclusiveness; yet they were
> also partly due, I fancy, to an uneasy sense
> that the particularism needed some religious
> veneer and justification, and partly to the
> higher, if inarticulate, feeling that the
> world exists for the sake of religion and the
> glory of God, and that religious truth is of
> ultimate and inexplicable value.[50]

As in all other examples, a positive virtue is again
found to extricate the Rabbis. The suggestion that the
Rabbis vulgarly held the Trinity to be a pagan belief is
modified by the view that the Rabbinic conception of God
was purer; the placing of God at home in the Temple itself
was mitigated by the concept of the *Shechinah*; God may be
cruel to Israel's enemies and He may favor the Jews too
much, but the Rabbis realized that the world exists for
the glory of God even if they erred in believing that they
were His chosen people. One last example of a love/hate
attitude on Montefiore's part, and the last of these examples, is the following:

> 6) But in how many O. T. passages are we told of
>   God's anger, of His jealousy, of His fierce
>   punishments! And the Rabbis had to regard all
>   such passages as also divine and accurate.
>   The Bible even seems to imply that God rejoices
>   at the destruction or death of the wicked. The
>   "natural man" of the Rabbis tended to acquiesce.
>   But attempts were made to rise above this con-
>   ception. The first part of the following pas-
>   sage is quoted in every anthology. It must
>   be confessed that it is isolated, but its in-
>   fluence was great:
>
>   (R. Johanan expressed that view that God
>   does not rejoice in the downfall of the wicked.)
>   The ministering angels wanted to sing a hymn
>   at the destruction of the Egyptians, but God
>   said: "My children lie drowned in the sea, and
>   you would sing? R. Elazar said: He does not
>   rejoice, but He causes others to rejoice.[51]

Clearly then Montefiore has great respect for Rabbinic ideas about God. These ideas he praises directly or their deficiencies are explained away or counterbalanced by positive aspects. Similarly, if Montefiore is less inclined than the Rabbis to love the Law, there were also aspects of their respect for it which he feels would be useful to Liberal Jews and Christians.

Our test samples in Montefiore's most famous book vindicate our central thesis. Montefiore is not the objective writer the Reverend Matthews would have us think he is. Montefiore has a definite point of view which is blatant or is easily inferred. He is willing to employ learning to advance a personal cause, he is even willing to distort the facts depending on audience and goal.

NOTES

CHAPTER III

[1]Schechter, *Some Aspects of Rabbinic Theology.*

[2]Moore, *Judaism in the First Centuries.*

[3]Arthur Cohen, *Everyman's Talmud* (New York: E. P. Dutton & Co., Inc., 1949).

[4]*A Rabbinic Anthology*, p. xii.

[5]Ibid.

[6]Ibid., p. lv.

[7]In Raphael Loewe's Prolegomenon to ibid.

[8]These are in his voluminous notes appended to the *Anthology* consisting of over 50 pages and for 23 pages of his Introduction which cite 16 major areas of disagreement.

[9]*A Rabbinic Anthology*, p. xvii.

[10]Ibid., p. lxx.

[11]Ibid.

[12]Ibid., p. lxxvi.

[13]Ibid., pp. lxxvi-lxxvii.

[14]Of the *Anthology*'s 31 chapters only one is devoted exclusively to the Rabbis' love of the Law, though possibly one or two others deal with it as a subordinate topic. By contrast, six full chapters are devoted directly to Rabbinic concerns about God (I--"The Nature and Character of God and His Relations with Man," II--"God's Love for Israel," III--"Man's Nature and God's Grace," IV--"Israel's Love for God," IX--"Divine Mercy and Divine Judgement...," X--"The Importance of Nature...and the Praise of God," XI--"Man's Repentance and God's Compassion") and virtually every other chapters reflects Rabbinic beliefs about God in one way or another.

[15]*A Rabbinic Anthology*, pp. xvi-xvii.

[16]Ibid., p. xxiv.

[17]Ibid., p. liv.

[18]Ibid., p. liii.

[19]Ibid., p. 119.

[20]Ibid., p. 132.

[21]Ibid., p. 137.

[22]Ibid., p. 156.

[23]Ibid., p. 124.

[24]Ibid., p. 126.

[25]Ibid., p. 130. This comment is called forth from *Tanh. B.*, Debarim 1a: "when God revealed His presence to the Israelites, He did not show forth all His goodness at once, because they could not have borne so much good," etc.

[26]Ibid. This is partly based on the following statement: "Resh Lakish said: There are times when the suppression [or cancellation] of the Torah [perhaps, rather 'of a commandment in the Torah'] may be the [firmer] foundation of Torah" (*Men.* 99b).

[27]Ibid., p. 165.

[28]Ibid., p. 167. The quotation which follows is from *Tanh. B.*, Yitro 38b: "God said to Israel, 'On this day I have given you the Law, and individuals toil at it, but in the world to come I will teach it to *all* Israel, and they will not forget it.'"

[29]This is not the only time Montefiore makes favorable comparisons between the Rabbis and the Greeks in the *Anthology*. There are, for instance, six references to Aristotle (and Loewe has one), seven to Plato, and five others to Greek or Hellenistic philosophy, ethics, etc., all of which are positive.

[30]*A Rabbinic Anthology*, p. 143. The Biblical verse is from Psalm 119. The Rabbinic comment is in *Psalms Midrash*.

[31]*A Rabbinic Anthology*, p. 148. My emphasis.

[32]Ibid., p. 157.

[33]*The Hibbert Lectures*, p. 169.

[34]*A Rabbinic Anthology*, p. xxvi.

[35]Ibid., p. xxvii.

[36]Ibid., p. xxviii.

[37]Ibid.

[38]Ibid.

[39]Ibid., p. xxxii.

[40]Ibid., pp. xxxii-xxxiii.

[41]Ibid., pp. xxxv-xxxvi.

[42]Ibid., p. xxvi.

[43]Ibid., p. xxxvi.

[44]Ibid., p. 7.

[45]Ibid., p. 15.

[46]Loewe took great exception to Montefiore's denunciation of sacrifice. For six and one half pages in his Introduction (pp. lxxxvi-xciii) and for six and one half pages in his notes (pp. 643-49) Loewe goes into great detail defending both the practice and the Rabbinic yearning for it, if not advocating its re-adoption in the future.

[47]Ibid., p. 15.

[48]Ibid., p. 24.

[49]Ibid., p. 38.

[50]Ibid., pp. 97-98.

[51]Ibid., p. 52.

CHAPTER IV

CONCLUSIONS

It remains to evaluate Montefiore's contribution to our understanding of the Rabbis. We have seen that because of the nature of the materials, and because of Montefiore's purposes, much of what he writes about the Talmud and its authors is uncomplimentary. On the other hand, because Montefiore perceives himself to be in the footsteps of the Rabbis, he frequently praises them and their endeavors.

We have also seen that a great deal of what Montefiore writes is polemical in nature. His comments on Rabbinic and other ancient religious thought are primarily designed to expound the teachings of Liberal Judaism. Montefiore speaks a great deal about "the truth" and no doubt sought it wherever he could. He was honest enough to give legitimate readings of the opposition's point of view before stating his own. However, what he produced in the end was not necessarily objective truth. This is not to suggest that Montefiore lied or was in any way dishonest. There is no evidence to substantiate such a claim. But in certain circumstances Montefiore ignored evidence or was blinded by the necessity of advancing his new religion. On some matters he never seemed able to make up his mind. We have seen several examples of how he would waver on the question of whether Jesus or the Rabbis first expressed opinions which were held in common. We have seen that Montefiore was not certain whether Greek influences were always good for Judaism, and we have seen him make vigorous, if not always successful, defenses of both positions. These ambivalences are the price he pays for keeping Liberal Judaism in the background of all he wrote. Every thought has as its motive the spreading of the new doctrine, not necessarily an accurate rendering of

73

the past. As a consequence, much of what he wrote distorted his subjects and their writings.

Another problem Montefiore presents to his readers results from the fact that he was not of the first generation of Reformers. His career began in 1892, more than five decades after Reform had reached its stride on the Continent and in Britain. He can thus assume that his readers are familiar with Reform's basic approach and so does not think it necessary to identify his sources. This may have made for smoother reading, but it does present the modern critic with the difficulty of having to assume that ideas similar to those of previous Reformers were indeed from those sources. In point of fact, they may have been or they may have been part of the general Jewish milieu, ideas so familiar by the time Montefiore wrote them that they could be taken as truth, or at least as often-heard arguments, with little or no concern as to their origins. Nevertheless, tracking down Montefiore's ideas was seen as essential to the flow of this study and an attempt has been made to do so where relevant. In sum, it was seen that Montefiore blended the techniques of *Wissenschaft des Judentums* and the ideas of Holdheim, Geiger, and Schechter, selecting what he thought viable from each; in much the same way he picked and chose from the Rabbis. Montefiore's truly novel additions to Judaism and to our understanding of the Rabbis are that *Halakhah* had *never* had any salvific value and that Greek philosophy and Christian morality must be absorbed into Judaism.

One last way he differs from the earlier Reformers is in his background. Geiger and Holdheim, for instance, had had a traditional Jewish upbringing. Montefiore did not. From his diary as a student and his letter to Cohen in 1925, we can assume that Montefiore, unlike his predecessors, had had Reformist tendencies from his youth. He apparently had always read the Rabbis with a preconceived bias, a bias which was reflected throughout his life. Starting as he did from an advanced position, Montefiore could then carry his ideas on the Rabbis much further than his predecessors whose horizons had been limited by their Orthodox training.

While many may disagree with Montefiore's attitudes, it would be wrong to dismiss the man, his understanding and his writings. The fact is that most of what he writes, for whatever reasons he writes it, is of benefit to the audience it is aimed at. Montefiore is concerned with the scholarly community, but he usually writes for laymen unfamiliar with, or unable to acquire, the writings of the Rabbis. When he puts what he thinks to be the core of the ancients' thoughts before this audience, he performs a notable and commendable task. That some of what he writes is marred by pre-conception is unfortunate but not unique, and most of what he has to say could be supported by the intellectual community of his day and of ours. What must be remembered by readers of Montefiore on the Rabbis is that, while the works are very valuable, they must be read with caution lest one learn more about the author than about his subjects. Montefiore's writings must be taken for what they are, not for what they might have been. He is not concerned with form criticism or with tracing the thoughts of individual Rabbis, nor is he concerned with how Rabbinical views changed over the centuries. Instead he seeks to present the totality of the Rabbis as an institution. He is interested in the end product, not in the way that product was fashioned. Most importantly, he is concerned to show how the ancient Rabbis can be used in the contemporary world. His goal is not to abandon the Rabbis, but to employ them in Reform. These being his aims, we can conclude that he succeeded.

BIBLIOGRAPHY

Bentwich, Norman. *Claude Montefiore and his Tutor in Rabbinics*. Southampton, England: University of Southampton, 1966).

Blau, Joseph. *Reform Judaism: A Historical Perspective*. New York: KTAV Publishing House, Inc., 1973.

Boman, Thorleif. *Hebrew Thought Compared with Greek*. New York: W. W. Norton & Company, Inc., 1970). Originally published in 1960.

Bonsirven, Joseph. *Palestinian Judaism in the Time of Jesus Christ*. New York: Holt, Rinehart and Winston, 1914.

Burkitt, F. C. "Claude Montefiore." *Speculum Religiones*. Oxford: Clarendon Press, 1929.

Cohen, Dr. Arthur. *Everyman's Talmud*. New York: E. P. Dutton and Co., Inc., 1949. Originally published 1931.

Cohen, Lucy. *Some Recollections of Claude Goldsmid Montefiore*. London: Faber and Faber, Ltd., 1940.

Geiger, Abraham. *Judaism and Its History*. New York: The Block Publishing Co., 1911.

Herford, Robert. *Christianity in Talmud and Midrash*. New York: KTAV Publishing House, Inc., 1975. Originally published in 1903.

Kaplan, Mordecai. *The Greater Judaism in the Making*. New York: The Reconstructionist Press, 1960.

Matthews, W. R. *Claude Montefiore: The Man and His Thought*. Southampton, England: University of Southampton, 1956.

Montefiore, Claude G. *The Bible for Home Reading*. London: Macmillan and Co., Ltd., 1925. Originally published 1896. 2 vols.

_____. *The Hibbert Lectures, 1892: Lectures on the Origin and Growth of Religion as Illustrated by the Religion of the Ancient Hebrews*. London: Williams and Norgate, 1893.

_____. *Judaism and St. Paul*. New York: Arno Press, 1973. Originally published 1914.

Montefiore, Claude G. *Liberal Judaism: An Essay*. London: Macmillan and Co., Ltd., 1903.

_____. *Liberal Judaism and Hellenism and other Essays*. London: Macmillan and Co., Ltd., 1918.

_____. *The Old Testament and After.* London: Macmillan and Co., Ltd., 1923.

_____. *Outlines of Liberal Judaism: For the Use of Parents and Teachers*. London: Macmillan and Co., Ltd., 1912.

_____ and Loewe, Herbert. *A Rabbinic Anthology*. New York: Schocken Books, Inc., 1974. Originally published 1938.

_____. *Rabbinic Literature and Gospel Teachings*. London: Macmillan and Co., Ltd., 1930.

_____. *Some Elements of the Religious Teachings of Jesus*. London: Macmillan and Co., Ltd., 1910.

_____. *The Synoptic Gospels*. New York: KTAV Publishing House, Inc., 1968. Originally published 1927. 2 vols.

_____. *Truth in Religion and other Sermons*. London: Macmillan and Co., Ltd., 1906.

Moore, George Foot. *Judaism in the First Centuries of the Christian Era: The Age of Tannaim*. Cambridge, MA: Harvard University Press, 1927, 1930. 3 vols.

Neusner, Jacob. *Aphrahat and Judaism: The Christian Jewish Argument in Fourth Century Iran*. Leiden: E. J. Brill, 1971.

_____. *Invitation to the Talmud*. New York: Harper and Row, 1973.

_____. *Rabbinic Traditions about the Pharisees Before 70*. Leiden: E. J. Brill, 1971.

Petuchowski, Jakob J. *Prayerbook Reform in Europe*. New York: The World Union for Progressive Judaism, Ltd., 1968.

Philipson, David. *The Reform Movement in Judaism*. New York: The Macmillan Co., 1931.

Plaut, W. Gunther. *The Rise of Reform Judaism*. New York: World Union for Progressive Judaism, Ltd., 1963.

Sandmel, Samuel. *We Jews and Jesus*. New York: Oxford University Press, 1965.

Schechter, Solomon. *Some Aspects of Rabbinic Theology*. New York: The Macmillan Co., 1910.

Schürer, Emil. *The Jewish People in the Time of Jesus Christ*. New York: Charles Scribner's Sons, 1898.

Stein, Leonard. *The Balfour Declaration*. New York: Simon and Schuster, 1961.

Tcherikover, Victor. *Hellenistic Civilization and the Jews*. Philadelphia: J.P.S.A., 1966.

52352